IT'S TIME TO l

ORIGINAL BLUEPRINT

10 STEPS TO
RE-DISCOVER
THE REAL
YOU & YOUR
PURPOSE

SONYIA GRAHAM

Colored Mirrors Publishing

Spring, Texas

It's Time to Uncover Your Original Blueprint

Library of Congress Control Number: 2018904010

ISBN: 978-1-732-1078-0-9 (Electronic)
ISBN: 978-1-732-1078-1-6 (Paperback)
ISBN: 978-1-732-1078-3-0 (Hardcover)

Book Design by Marvin D. Cloud

Colored Mirrors Publishing books may be ordered through booksellers or by contacting:

Colored Mirrors Publishing, LLC.
4008 Louetta Road, Ste 193
Spring, TX 77388

www.coloredmirrorspublishing.com

Printed in the USA

It's Time to Uncover Your Original Blueprint

10 Steps to Re-discover the Real You & Your Purpose

To Lynn,
Live your best
life on purpose.
Love,
Tenyjua M. Graham,
your home girl :)

ENDORSEMENTS

"This book is a result of 11 years of growth and change that has prepared Sonyia Graham to be the testimony and glory of God made manifest. I love the Spirit-filled presence over the words and how educational as well relatable it is for many of us. I pray that more and more people can benefit from her words and experiences."
—**Noah Hagihasani, Houston, TX**

"*It's Time to Uncover Your Original Blueprint* is an amazing book that everyone should read. Not only does it give you practical applications that you can use in your life, but it gives you biblical sources to help guide you. Pick up your copy today."
—**Nia Abdallah, Olympian**

"*It's Time to Uncover Your Original Blueprint* is an excellent and relevant read for those who hunger and thirst for their understanding of their divine purpose!"
—**Clarence P. Landry, Houston, TX**

"Your book, *It's Time to Uncover Your Original Blueprint*, is ageless. This book is a great teaching tool for churches, religious schools, and social organizations. The activities, ideas, strategies, and suggestions are resources that support the developmental core values that you can live by on a daily basis and throughout your life. What you have created can make a difference for those who take your messages to heart, male and female."
—**Kittie Weston-Knauer, BMX Champion**

One Life

You only get one life. Who is living yours?
Don't you think it's time you got to know them?

Sonyia Graham

DEDICATION

I dedicate this book to my mother, Carol Ann Thompson, who at the age of 17, God chose to give me life. She sacrificed her youth and pledged her life to be an amazing mother of four children. Life was not easy, but the abundance of her love made up for any lack. She has the biggest heart, a sweet spirit, truly loves God and people. Her devotion and faith are unwavering even in her daily dealings with multiple sclerosis. She doesn't complain and always has a smile on her face. Mom, you are my role model and the virtuous woman, I strive to be. Your strength has given me life, and you are the wind beneath my wings. Thank you for your love and for helping me become the woman I am today.

ACKNOWLEDGMENTS

It's Time to Uncover Your Original Blueprint would not have the spirit it has without the invaluable academic, educational, psychological, and human support and belief in me as a writer and researcher.

I have provided you with meaningful information and strategies in *It's Time to Uncover Your Original Blueprint* to help you understand better, (10 Steps to Re-discover the Real You and Your Purpose). Don't miss it!

Firstly, my profound gratitude and sincere thanks to Almighty God for his vision, support, and guidance on this journey and throughout the research. His continued help leads me in the right way.

I would like to extend my indebtedness to my parents, Carol and Jimmy Thompson, and Herman Baring; my children, Andrew Graham and Victoria Graham; my BFF, Ilona Ransom; my siblings who have been a part of this process, Marlene Baring, Ric Baring, Mark Baring and Demetrius Thompson; all of my other siblings; my grandmother, Deloris Davis; my aunt, Terri Walton; my uncles, Gary Baring, Butch Williams, Tony Williams, and Marquis Williams; Pastor William J. Lindsey, D. Min., Clarence P. Landry and Dr. D. Ivan Young for their advice during the research. Without their encouragement, I would not have had the chance to complete this book.

And to my family and friends, I acknowledge my heartfelt appreciation for their valuable guidance, constant encouragement, and untiring help which has been a source of inspiration at all stages of the work during this journey.

CONTENTS

PART 3: Live Your Best Life

FOREWORD

If you are in doubt about your original blueprint, your uncertainties are over. In *It's Time to Uncover Your Original Blueprint*, Sonyia Graham has penned an epic book with a relevant action plan that will change the trajectory of your life. The author wrote this blueprint in an engaging and captivating style with the right balance of intellectual information with practical advice.

Sonyia Graham is convinced that humans can uncover their original blueprint. In this inspiring book, Graham writes a simple yet richly endowed framework to do so. From Graham's life experiences, challenges, and walk with God, she has designed a blueprint process in a format that is easy to understand and apply. The author explains the concepts in this book from her viewpoint. Sonyia Graham is one of the kindest people you will ever meet. She has a heart to see people living what God designed for their lives. I've seen her use the tools in this book to help reframe and rebuild her life. She writes from her expertise and experience. After years of research, Graham has given us tools that aid in implementing and achieving your original blueprint goals; it's like steroids for goal setting.

By the time you finish reading this book, woven with Scriptures and wisdom, you will uncover and discover the original blueprint for your life. Read it multiple times and allow Graham's passion to encourage you with an optimistic perspective on not missing out of the purpose of your original blueprint. This book is a wealth of information; each chapter packs a punch! This book is timeless!

I highly recommend It's *Time to Uncover Your Original Blueprint* to help you navigate to your original God-designed blueprint to a better life.

—William J. Lindsey, D. Min.
Author of *The Will To Be: Becoming More Than You Are*

INTRODUCTION

What is Passive Assimilation?

Passive Assimilation is an Unspoken Silent Epidemic

1. passive
   Accepting or allowing what happens without active response or resistance.
2. assimilate
   To become like something; to mimic or copy

Passive assimilation, therefore, is to mimic or copy something (or someone) without resistance to become like it (them). Passive assimilation is also a silent epidemic—one in which a person gets lost in someone else's dreams, aspirations, and purpose while sacrificing their own. And in the process of doing so, that person's sense of self-worth shrinks or even disappears.

Even worse, sometimes the person doesn't even realize what is taking place. Others, however, do recognize but choose to be silent. Those of us who are silently passively assimilative usually maintain that silence for one of two reasons:

- We are too embarrassed to tell anyone. We believe we are alone—that we are the only ones with this problem when the reality is that far too many of us are in this 'boat'.
- We wish to avoid confrontation at all cost— even when the price is so steep and so personal.

While the problem of passive assimilation isn't always severe, some of us have never learned the importance of carving out our own existence or have never received the understanding that people are created for a unique set of purposes. Or ... somewhere along the way we have forgotten the importance of our individual existence and the importance of living the life we were created by God to live by being the person He destined us to be. We have, to some extent or another, forgotten that each of us has our own purpose. To help remind you of this, let's look at a couple of verses in the Bible that indicate how special and unique we are:

"For we are God's handiwork, created in Christ Jesus to do good works, which God prepared in advance for us to do"
(Ephesians 2:10 NIV).

"The Lord will fulfill his purpose for me; your steadfast love, O Lord, endures forever. Do not forsake the work of your hands"
(Psalm 138.8 ESV).

Some of the most common reasons for losing sight of our unique self is a relationship, marriage or responsibilities. Far too many of us erroneously allow our identity to be blanketed or even smothered out by our mates. This is incredibly sad, and in marriage, it is NOT how God intended marriage to be. Look…

"That is why a man leaves his father and mother and is united to his wife, and they become one flesh" (Genesis 2:24 NIV).

United … becoming one flesh. This doesn't mean one is more valuable or important than the other. Not at all! To be united and one means to complement each other and bring out the best in each other.

"However, each one of you also must love his wife as he loves himself, and the wife must respect her husband" (Ephesians 5:33 NIV).

Love, respect, treating one another as you want to be treated … I don't see anything about passive assimilation there, do you? Even the verses that come before and after verse thirty-three that talk about submission, aren't promoting giving up your identity. Submission isn't about inferiority and having a subservient mindset. Submission is recognizing and embracing the different roles God has assigned to us as husbands and wives so that we don't lose sight of our intended purpose ... our original blueprint.

Clearly, both our individual purpose and marriage are important to God, so it only makes sense that in His infinite wisdom He gave us the power to enjoy and succeed in both.

Even knowing that still leaves us with the question of why, in a relationship, do we often feel the need to give up one to have the other—only to look in the mirror one day wondering who we are and where our former self-went? When exactly did it happen ... and why did we let it happen?

Now what were simple questions to answer in the past are now hard for you to answer, such as:

1. What do you like to do?
2. Where would you like to go?
3. What would you like to have?
4. What would you like to be?
5. What are your dreams for yourself?

At least they are hard to answer when it comes to yourself. But not surprisingly, you probably have all the answers to these questions for others (mate, children, etc.), but not for yourself. Taking it a step farther, you probably haven't given these questions much thought regarding you. In fact, until now you quite possibly thought you were living your own life and working toward your dreams. Or maybe a correct way to say it would be: you assumed you were living the life you are meant to live because, in the process of living, somehow your loved ones' goals and dreams have become yours. Willingly or unwillingly … consciously or subconsciously you have conceded your life's purpose away.

You had the best intentions while allowing this to take place. You wanted this relationship so badly, despite all the red flags you refused to acknowledge because you thought it was more important to make sure everyone else was happy and to avoid as much friction as possible. In your mind, you convinced yourself that your sacrifice would be appreciated and that eventually, it would all be worth it. But that's not what happened. Instead of being viewed as someone who is capable, intelligent, and worthy of honor and respect, you made yourself out to appear weak, indecisive, and incapable in the eyes of your mate and children. Believe it or not, seeing you in this light sometimes can make these same people come to resent you and lose a level of respect for you or feel sorry for you. They see you as a victim, but a victim by choice. Keep in mind many times it is you that has set the tone for this in your relationships.

Be who you are and say what you feel, because those who mind don't matter, and those who matter don't mind.
—Bernard Baruch

These actions can also plant seeds of resentment in you because you begin feeling undervalued and unappreciated despite all your sacrifices. Unfortunately, your family members are correct—you are a victim by choice. You chose to give up your own identity. Your reasons were noble—just misguided.

At this point, you are probably thinking, *What are you talking about? I am the one who is voiceless, taken for granted, unappreciated, unvalued that has sacrificed for everyone else!*

Sorry, I can only empathize with you rather than offer sympathy because sympathy, which means I feel sorry for you, is not going to help you change things. Empathy, which leads to a compassionate response can, if you let it. So, it is with complete empathy that I want to help you acknowledge and take responsibility for your role in allowing these things to happen in your life. And understand that when you do, you will then be holding the key to the 'door' that opens to the road of your healing.

Only when you possess this key will you be able to rediscover and move forward toward your original blueprint and the purposes for your life as God intended. Taking this critical step will also help ensure you don't return to the unfulfilling, self-deprecating place of passive assimilation. After all, when we know better, we should do better. It is crucial that you understand the responsibility you have to your children. Show them and teach them the importance of realizing who they are and the importance of becoming confident in their purpose before approaching a relationship. They should continue to live out those purposes while in a relationship.

Jeremiah 1:5 (NLT) says: "I knew you before I formed you in your mother's womb. Before you were born I set you apart and appointed you as my prophet to the nations." In teaching your children by example to live this way, you will be doing your part to stop the epidemic of passive assimilation. And my friends, we must stop this epidemic … now!

When I started writing this book, I believed the targeted audience would be women. That seemed only logical to me because the issue we are talking about is much more common among women than it is among men. But the more I came to understand this epidemic and the more research I did, I came to the realization that gender has nothing to do with it. What determines whether someone becomes a victim of this epidemic is the role a person—male or female—chooses to take in their relationship. That being said, this is not a relationship-bashing book. It is a book written to promote self-re-discovery, self-empowerment, and self- awareness in partnership with God. Through the interactive exercises and tools provided, it is my goal to help you move in a positive direction so that you can experience life with fulfillment and joy the way YOU are meant to experience it.

This Can Happen to Anyone

Becoming passively assimilated sort of creeps up on you; usually happening over the course of time without you even realizing what is taking place. And then one day you understand life isn't what you want it to be. You know that somewhere along the way the real you got lost. But how? How did it happen ... and why?

Here are the answers to those questions: You ignored the warning signs of passive assimilation. Don't be too hard on yourself, though. It's easy to do. Think about it—if it weren't so easy, it wouldn't be such a huge problem.

To get yourself out of this situation, you will need to recognize and acknowledge that you may have allowed any combination of the following:

- For the sake of not putting the relationship at risk, you did not provide honest feedback that expressed your true feelings, likes, and   dislikes in the early stages of the relationship. Since it worked, you maintained the status quo to keep the relationship going.
- You gave up your job for the good of the family; making you feel as though you had lost leverage in the relationship. Doing so also made you devalue your self-worth and led you to reclassify yourself as a dependent.
- You allowed your mate to assume the parent role over you and you responded in obedience.
- You allowed someone to carve you into what they wanted you to be or fix you even though you were not broken.
- You traded in your dreams and aspirations for someone else's.
- You were too accessible and did not bring your own life or existence into the relationship.
- You wanted the relationship badly enough that you were willing to do whatever it took to make it work, even if it meant compromising your values.
- You had not defined who you were prior to the relationship, so you did not have anything to hold on to.
- You forgot that you only have one life to live.
- You forgot you already had a purpose in life long before you took on titles like Wife/Husband,

Doctor, Teacher, and Mother/Father.
- You may have been tempted or lured by material security.
- You stopped doing some of the things you enjoyed before or during the early stages of the relationship (going to church, hobbies, spending time with family and friends) so your mate did not know this was part of who you were.

You may not control all the events that happen to you, but you can decide not to be reduced by them.

—Maya Angelou

PART 1: MY JOURNEY

What a journey it has been. In this section, you will see that sometimes even the clearest paths can take unexpected turns. You will also learn why it is important to keep moving forward even in times of uncertainty. Remember you have to get to it, to get through it. A journey takes motion. Keep moving; you will get there.

CHAPTER 1
BIRTH OF "WHO AM I?"

IT ALL BEGAN IN October of 2006 when I was invited to participate in a Susan Komen Breast Cancer walk with a friend. The weather was perfect—sunny but not too hot or humid. I could even feel a light cool breeze hitting my face from time to time, and I remember thinking to myself how blessed we were to have this kind of weather in Houston in October.

I guess I was especially mindful of how beautiful the weather was because it was the opposite of the Octobers I experienced growing up in Des Moines, Iowa. Having such a picturesque autumn day was something I counted as a blessing. It could also have been the fact that the Susan G Komen walk is an important event for me. I, like countless others, have lost loved ones to breast cancer, so walking and raising money for a cure is something I take seriously.

As I walked, it also brought back memories of the 3-day 60-mile Avon Breast Cancer Walk I did some years earlier in honor of my cousin, Gordette Brown and many others. That experience was spiritual and empowering for me. Walking from LEGOLAND in Carlsbad, CA to SeaWorld in San Diego, CA was something I will never forget. We walked an average of 20 miles per day, pitched a tent every night when it came time to go to bed, and showered inside a semi-truck retrofitted with showers for the event. But the most amazing part of all was meeting women from all over the country who traveled there to be a part of this worthwhile cause. While walking past some of the most beautiful terrain and scenic views, I could not help but gaze out in awe over the sea of women united for trying to save lives. This event gave me a newfound perspective of just how strong, passionate, and powerful women are and that we were created that way for a purpose. Most of all, I saw more clearly than ever that we have a voice and presence in this world, but we are far too willing to harness or suppress that voice.

That was my great take away from that weekend. The not-so-good take away was shin splints. Living in ultra-flat Houston, Texas, it was not possible for me to train for the hills and inclines that I called mountains in California. But, shin splints and all, it was incredibly worth it.

But that's enough of my digressing. Let's go back to the walk I was on that October day of 2006. I felt that same sense of pride all over again. I also re-experienced the same spiritual reminders that women are meant to exhibit the passion, strength, and courage we were created to possess.

During this walk, I had a very heartfelt conversation with my dear friend, Leslie. The crazy part was that this conversation played out like a record repeating itself, like it was stuck in the same spot. This discussion was the same one I seemed to be hearing from almost all of my friends and women colleagues.

How was it possible that we all seemed to be at the same place in our lives - feeling as though we had lost our sense of purpose and identity? At first, I felt a sense of relief come over me because I knew I was not by myself. Immediately after that, though, I was sad because at that moment I was sure this problem was bigger than we were. I thought back to the sea of women and wondered how many of those powerful, ambitious women alongside me that I had mentioned before were unaware of their struggle with this epidemic as well. And that is when my mind started wandering; thinking about all the people, men, and women alike, who have lost sight of themselves.

Next, I began to analyze the situation in my mind. At that time, it seemed like most of the issues were marriage-related, so I named the issue, "Where is the ME in marriage?" After the walk, I rushed home to talk to my best friend, Ilona and discuss this theory. The initial thought was that women needed to have a platform to voice these feelings and a place of support, so they would know they are not alone. It sounded like a great project to work on—one that excited me. But then I realized I needed to go through my own re-discovery to develop the tools and steps of self-rediscovery to be qualified to share this with others.

Even though I strongly felt that God said this was supposed to be a book and to travel and share this platform worldwide, I said, "Absolutely not!"

Me standing in front of people doing that? I don't think so! So instead Ilona and I worked very hard to create a website platform instead. We even got friends together to do focus groups to gather feedback on what they wanted to see on the website. We were moving toward a woman's socially interactive website like Facebook that would include the things that interest women (parenting, travel, shopping and me time). Ilona even learned how to do HTML/Joomla or something to assist in creating the website. It was a beautiful site with lots of bells and whistles. However, we never got it to do what we envisioned. I later came to realize that doing it your way and not God's, only delays the plan, it does not change it. He still was requiring what He purposed for this platform.

CHAPTER 2
MY JOURNEY BEGINS

THIS JOURNEY TOOK 11 years. During this time, I learned more about myself than I would have thought to be possible. I also gained a better understanding of what I called the epidemic of passive assimilation and how it happens. More accurately stated, I learned that passive assimilation doesn't just happen. We are not victims. We do it to ourselves. We must take ownership of the role we play in letting our true selves disappear. Coming to these realizations was my first step toward healing, change, and acceptance. It must be yours, as well. The next step for me was to begin re-discovering myself and seeking happiness by realizing that I have my own life and that I was created with my own purpose.

I am thankful for this journey. I have grown so much, and I am still experiencing the fruits of what has transpired over these past 11 years. I am also thankful for the perfectness of God's timing in all of it. Had this book been published in 2006, it would have been a husband-bashing, mob and pitchfork inducing kind of book—not at all like the one you are about to read. Back in 2006, I would have to say I agreed with the common thought process, that marriage is the culprit when it comes to identity theft (not the credit card kind). But that's not true. The truth of the matter is that an individual's unhappiness and displeasure with themselves can also put them in a position that allows their marriage or relationship to eat away at their identity.

You often see this in relationships with people around their thirties and up. They start wondering *what if* and grieve what they haven't yet done with their life. These feelings can morph into a sense of emptiness, and they start to disconnect from themselves emotionally. They no longer believe they know what inspires them and are certain they don't have anything to look forward to. Pretty soon these people are no longer dreaming and no longer aspiring to set or meet goals.

Sound familiar? You may feel like you, personally, have disappeared and that your existence is dependent upon the role you play in other's lives. You may even feel something is wrong with you—especially if you feel lost and invisible in spite of the fact that you have all the things society says should make you happy: healthy, well-adjusted children, a picture-perfect marriage or at the very least, one that seems to be working, a home, cars, careers, education, etc. Society says you should feel great, but you don't. And the guilt you feel from not feeling great only serves to make a bad situation even worse.

NO GOING BACK

The one thing I can tell you I learned on this journey is that once you understand this epidemic and begin to work through this whole process, you will never be the same. The person you once called you, before the discovery, will no longer exist. You won't be able to go back to behaving like that person, even if you want to. And trust me, you won't want to.

There will be some areas in your life you will need to re-negotiate. Your new-found self will go from not having goals and dreams, to looking forward to and being excited about what life has to offer. You will find yourself wanting to make the most of your life by finding and fulfilling your purpose.

No longer will your answers to life questions revolve around your family's hopes, dreams, and aspirations instead of those things deep within your heart. You will even be able to think past others' needs and wants, to your own needs and wants. Your conversations with others will begin to include you and what's going on in your life.

The critical thing to realize is that everyone was created for a specific 'set of purposes'. It is now time for you to take your place in this world by doing what you were created to do. Somewhere along my journey of getting to this point in writing this book, I realized that the title *Where Is the ME …* only addressed the problem, but what we needed was an answer in the form of a solution, with a sense of urgency. *It's Time to Uncover Your Original Blueprint* is that solution.

I want to thank my best friend, Ilona Ransom for being on this journey of re-discovery with me right from the start. I thank her for believing in me and supporting my efforts through content contribution, research, sharing her life experiences, and for being a constant source of encouragement (just to name a few).

When God gave me the vision for this book 11 years ago, he said to write it and share it by way of speaking to others and create a platform that will help redirect others who have lost themselves and give them the tools needed to help them find their way back to their purpose. The other facet is to reach the young people and show them they are fearfully and wonderfully made. I am writing *Staying True to Your Original Blueprint Workbook* and *Journaling Through Your Original Blueprint* for this reason. Once we understand that the Lord uniquely made us the way we are for a specific purpose. This also gives us peace and clarity in knowing that we do not have to succumb to the pressure of being like other people. Simply put- If God wanted us to be like others He would have created us that way.

"I will praise thee; for I am fearfully and wonderfully made; marvellous are thy works; and that my soul knoweth right well" (Psalm 139:14 KJV).

Finally, it is important that you know God loves us unconditionally. He created us with our own purpose, and that purpose is perfect for us not because we chose it, but because God chose us to fulfill it. That makes us qualified. Even with our confusion, fear, and self-doubt, it is already decided we have to trust God and have faith.

Psalm 119:105 (NIV) says His word is the lamp for my feet, a light on my path.

This is why it is essential to develop and understand your own self-worth and importance of not letting go of it. God also wanted me to go out and speak to those whose identities are still intact especially the young people. But I thought to myself, *not me!* I was not about to stand up in front of groups of people...talking, I couldn't do that!

Instead, I decided to try to compromise with God by creating an amazing website to help get this message out. But this was not God's will for the vision, so it was not living up to its full potential. Then God blessed me with a job that I was not looking for, and it forced me to develop and use my public speaking skills. I couldn't help but see this as God's way of preparing me to be able to go out and speak about this book and platform. Only when I decided to do God's will for the book — to take the message to others in person — that it all started coming together.

I know there is still a lot of room for improvement in my speaking skills, but I can honestly say I am no longer afraid to step in front of a crowd. In fact, I look forward to it because I realize it is part of my purpose and His will for my life, and that it is necessary to help others. This book is my way to give God glory for blessing me with this fantastic opportunity. Besides, He has given me the vision and provision for it.

VISION

"Where there is no vision, the people perish: but he that keepeth the law, happy is he" (Proverbs 29:18 KJV).

"And the Lord answered me: "Write the vision; make it plain on tablets, so he may run who reads it" (Habakkuk 2:2 ESV).

"And the Lord said to Paul one night in a vision, 'Do not be afraid but go on speaking and do not be silent'" (Acts 18:9 ESV).

PROVISION

"And God is able to make all grace abound toward you; that ye, always having all sufficiency in all things, may abound to every good work" (2 Corinthians 9:8 KJV).

"And my God will supply every need of yours according to his riches in glory in Christ Jesus" (Philippians 4:19 ESV).

YOU ARE NOT READY

Three years ago, I had the opportunity to team up and meet Dr. D. Ivan Young, Certified Celebrity Relationship Expert and published author of several books. We talked about my book and my journey. I told him I was in the process of finishing my book. He said the book sounds great but, I was not ready to finish it. I was perplexed by his statement and became a bit defensive about it. He then graciously explained that until I made my own full transition in my journey, I would not have the material I needed to finish it. He said by completing the book at that time in my journey, I was merely one of the people I was trying to help. And honestly who needs to read about someone else's pain without a solution when they have their own?

He said once I finished my transition, I would have a solution, tools, and a testimony to help people and change lives. On this journey, I have met some great people who have given me support, direction and shared their trials and experiences with this epidemic. I have had countless passionate conversations with mere strangers about this topic over the years and the response is always incredible. My daughter has told me on numerous occasions how in awe she is with watching these conversations evolve into such bonds with strangers and the excitement they all convey about the opportunity to read this book to learn more about this epidemic.

I am thankful to say, I completed my journey over a year ago and Dr. Young was 100% right. I was not ready three years ago. I am grateful for the guardian angels

God sent in my path to help bring this gift He trusted me with to fruition. I am proud to say that writing the finale was a great joy and that in this new chapter of my life, I now look forward to traveling the world and sharing my journey. It evolved from a husband bashing to an awakening of acceptance of contribution, self-examination, self-discovery, redirection, transition, and a greater relationship with my Father God. My prayer is that this book will be a blessing to you and help you live your best life on God's purpose for you.

"For I can do everything through Christ, who
gives me strength"
(Philippians 4:13 NLT).

And so, can you ...

CHAPTER 3
YOUR LIFE, GOD'S PURPOSE

WE ALL HAVE A purpose and a destiny upon our lives whether we know it or not. Our purpose is to fulfill the will of God upon our lives but to do that we have to know what the will of God is and then begin to walk in it. We all have a purpose to fulfill here on the earth. To know Him and His Son Jesus Christ is step number one. There is no use going on to the next step if we haven't first made Jesus Lord in our lives. If we try to fulfill the will of God without first knowing God we will be walking in our own vanity, and we will not fulfill God's purpose, nor will we ever be fulfilled ourselves.

After this, there is the fulfilling of God's general Word. In other words, walking in the general purpose, God has given to all believers learning to walk in the power of the Word and follow the Holy Spirit of God. We will not get far if we do not know the Word of God and follow His Holy Spirit. Every believer also has a specific calling God has called him or her to fulfill.

Is having a purpose just a cliché? Or is it really something predestined for your life?

"In Him, we were also chosen, having predestined
according to the plan of Him who works out
everything in conformity with the purpose of
His will"
(Ephesians 1:11).

Some things have become whimsical in thought or
regurgitated by others, and we repeat what is popular.
If that's where you are when you think about your
purpose, think about what the Bible says about it.

Everyone was born with a purpose.

"But I have raised you up for this very purpose, that I
might show you my power and that my name might
be proclaimed in all the earth"
(Exodus 9:16).

Even through ups and downs, God fulfills His
purpose.

"And we know that in all things God works for the
good of those who love him, who have been called
according to his purpose"
(Romans 8:28).

Our salvation is only a part of God's purpose. His purpose is greater than merely saving us. Why not start out every morning asking God what is His will for your life?

"He has saved us and called us to a holy life—not because of anything we have done but because of his own purpose and grace"
(2 Timothy 1:9).

God fulfills His purpose through His children.

"Therefore, my dear friends, as you have always obeyed—not only in my presence but now much more in my absence—continue to work out your salvation with fear and trembling, for it is God who works in you to will and to act in order to fulfill his good purpose"
(Philippians 2:12-13).

God's Purpose will last.

"Many are the plans in a person's heart, but it is the Lord's purpose that prevails"
(Proverbs 19:21).

God's Purpose cannot be stopped or undone.

"I know that you can do all things; no purpose of
yours can be thwarted"
(Job 42:2).

Walking in your purpose can be scary. Maybe you
are still looking or waiting for God to show you your
purpose. Or perhaps He has already shown you your
purpose. Is that one not good enough? It is good enough;
now you need to trust that you are good enough for it.

Faith is trusting the future even if you can't see it. He
holds your future. He is waiting for you to trust Him and
follow Him to get there. You have nothing to lose if you
take your steps with faith. But you have everything to
lose if you die without that purpose being birthed. How
dare you waste God's gifts! He loves and treasures you.
He gave His only son for you. Do not let fear cripple you
and keep you from your dreams and purpose.

God tells us in these powerful Scriptures why we
need not fear.

"I prayed to the Lord, and he answered me.
He freed me from all my fears"
(Psalm 34:4 NLT).

"So do not fear, for I am with you; do not be
dismayed, for I am your God. I will strengthen you

and help you; I will uphold you with my righteous
right hand"
(Isaiah 41:10 NIV).

"The Lord is my light and my salvation -
whom shall I fear?
The Lord is the stronghold of my life - of whom shall I
be afraid?"
(Psalm 27:1 NIV).

"Even though I walk through the darkest valley, I will
fear no evil, for you are with me; your rod and your
staff, they comfort me"
(Psalm 23:4 NIV).

"Be strong and courageous. Do not be afraid or
terrified because of them, for the Lord your God goes
with you; he will never leave you nor forsake you"
(Deuteronomy 31:6 NIV).

We can see He is with us every step of the way. We
need to trust and lean on Him to guide our steps and
allow His will to be done here on earth as it is in heaven.
God wants us to live our best lives now. He needs us to
prepare this place and His people for His return.

"But seek first his kingdom and his righteousness,
and all these things will be given to you as well"
(Matthew 6:33 NIV)

> "For we are His workmanship, created in Christ
> Jesus for good works, which God prepared
> beforehand that we should walk in them"
> (Ephesians 2:10).

The Word of God is saying through the Apostle Paul that before God created the world, God ordained specific good works for us to walk in. He knows the beginning and the end, and He knows what we are supposed to do in our time here.

> "And if you call on the Father, who without
> partiality judges according to each one's work,
> conduct yourselves throughout the time of your
> sojourning here in fear"
> (1 Peter 1:17).

You might say, "I don't know what I am supposed to be doing. I am not called into ministry." We are not all called to the five-fold ministry: Apostle, Prophet, Pastor, Evangelist, and Teacher. We are called to good works. As Paul said to the Ephesians, we were created in Christ Jesus for good works before the world was created. God expects us to fulfill our calling on Earth, and He will hold us accountable. Our reward in eternity will be based on what we do with what He has given us now. That is not to be confused with our salvation. Salvation cannot be earned by works.

"Not by works of righteousness which we have done,
but according to His mercy He saved us, through the
washing of regeneration and renewing of
the Holy Spirit"
(Titus 3:5).

As the Apostle Peter said, we will be judged
according to our works so we must conduct our time
of sojourning here. Sojourning means we are passing
through. We must do something while we are on our
way to something else. We are not just occupying time
and space. Jesus talked about this in the parable of the
talents. Matthew 25:14-31(KJV) states:

> "For the kingdom of heaven is like a man
> travelling to a far country, who called his own
> servants and delivered his goods to them. And
> to one he gave five talents, to another two and to
> another one, to each according to his own ability;
> and immediately he went on a journey. Then
> he who had received the five talents went and
> traded with them and made another five talents.
> And likewise, he who had received two gained
> two more also. But he who had received one
> went and dug in the ground and hid his lord's
> money. After a long time, the Lord of the servants
> came and settled accounts with them. So, he
> who received five talents came and brought five
> other talents, saying, Lord, you delivered to me
> five talents; look, I have gained five more talents
> besides them. His lord said to him, "Well done,
> good and faithful servant; you were faithful over

31

a few things, I will make you ruler over many things. Enter into the joy of your lord." He also who had received two talents came and said, Lord, you delivered to me two talents; look, I have gained two more talents besides them. His lord said to him, "Well done, good and faithful servant; you have been faithful over a few things, I will make you ruler over many things. Enter into the joy of your lord." Then he who had received the one talent came and said, Lord, I knew you to be a hard man, reaping where you have not sown and gathered where you have not scattered seed. And I was afraid and went and hid your talent in the ground. Look, there you have what is yours. But his lord answered and said to him, "You wicked and lazy servant, you knew that I reap where I have not sown and gather where I have not scattered seed. Therefore, you ought to have deposited my money with the bankers, and at my coming, I would have received back my own with interest. Therefore, take the talent from him, and give it to him who does not have, even what he has will be taken away. And cast the unprofitable servant into the outer darkness. There will be weeping and gnashing of teeth. When the Son of Man comes in His glory, and all the holy angels with Him, then He will sit on the throne of His glory."

Each of them received talents according to their own ability. Or we could say it like this: Each person receives the grace to accomplish what God has for them to achieve. No one was given an unfair burden and asked to do more than they were capable of doing. We must perform what God has placed in our hand to accomplish. Maybe you are called to work with children or be a teacher. If that's the case, take the talents God has given you and use them to build up the next generation. This is just one example, but you can use your own judgment and see for yourself that it takes the entire body of Christ, to walk as a whole person. We can fulfill God's purpose individually, but we must also fulfill God's purpose collectively. I can't do it all any more than someone else. I can only do what I have been graced to do. If I don't do my part, then this puts a greater burden on someone else to do more than they are supposed to do. When that happened in the parable of the talents, what was given to the unprofitable servant was taken away and given to someone who had more. This should not only be a warning to us but also encourage us to reach out and fulfill the calling God has given each of us.

Because of God's grace, there is no need to fear, but I want to help encourage people who have never given much thought to this to begin to seek God and find His purpose for their life. Have a willing and obedient attitude. Be open to the leading of the Holy Spirit and you will see God's clear direction unfold before you. Be willing to step out and go wherever the Lord leads. He's not going to ask you to do something you are not capable or ready to do. He knows more than we do, and we can trust His judgment.

David was a good example of this. God said through the writer of Acts that David was a man after God's own heart.

"And when He had removed him, He raised up for them David as king, to whom also He gave testimony and said, I have found David the son of Jesse, a man after my own heart, who will do all My will; 'From this man's seed, according to the promise, God raised up for Israel a Savior Jesus'"
(Acts 13:22).

David was just a young boy herding sheep, yet God said he was a man after His own heart who would do all His will. David was in the back of the pasture herding sheep, yet his heart sought after God, and he had a desire to fulfill the purpose of God in his life. God didn't choose him randomly. David was a willing servant and later became an obedient servant. David messed up many times yet he was willing to repent when he messed up and go on regardless of the consequences. God not only used him, but his lineage became the lineage of the King of kings and the Lord of lords. He was a man after God's own heart, but the end of verse 22 says "he will do all my will." David fulfilled God purpose in his life by doing all of God's will. They go hand in hand. When you fulfill God's will, you will also fulfill your calling and destiny. That may sound like an obvious statement, however, many Christians miss the obvious. They seek after career choices never considering what God has for them. If God has called you to be an accountant, then you will never be happy teaching, and if you are called to teach, you will never be happy as an accountant.

God has placed something in each one of us to fulfill not only generally but specifically as well. No one else can tell you what your purpose is but if you will spend quiet time in God's presence and listen to His voice you will know, and God's peace will be there to confirm the direction He has given you.

God wants us to succeed; He doesn't want us to fail. He has called us all to be happy and prosperous, but if we are unwilling or disobedient, we won't accomplish what He has given us to accomplish. We all must start somewhere. Start where you are now. You can repent of the past if you have messed up and start fresh right now.

It takes both a willing and obedient heart to fulfill God's plan and purpose for your life.

"If you are willing and obedient, you shall eat the good of the land;"
(Isaiah 1:19).

The Lord spoke this Scripture to me many years ago when I was at a crossroads in my life. I was caught up in a situation that was not my choice, and I had no control over. Because of this, I started to get a bad attitude about it. I didn't realize it at the time, but a bitter attitude crept up on me slowly. When the Lord spoke this to me, I had been praying for peace. I knew in the natural that it wasn't likely, but I prayed and asked in faith and believed in faith. When the Lord spoke this Scripture to me, I realized the attitude problem I had and immediately repented. I changed my attitude immediately, and my whole outlook changed as well.

Because of this, the Lord blessed me with a fresh outlook on that situation and peace. I can now look back and see that this changed the course of my life. It would never have happened if I did not have a relationship with the Lord and had I not repented and turned into a willing as well as an obedient vessel.

Remember what the Prophet Isaiah said, "the willing and obedient will eat the good of the land." We must all have a willing heart and be obedient to the general as well as the specific call on our lives. Amen?

Do you know Jesus as your Lord and Savior? Do you want to be a joint heir with Christ? If so, I urge you to pray the following prayer earnestly.

Dear Heavenly Father, I come to you in the name of Jesus. Your word says, "and the one who comes to me, I will by no means cast out" (John 6:37). So, I know you won't cast me out, but you take me in, And I thank you for it. You said in your Word, "whoever calls upon the name of the Lord shall be saved" (Romans. 10:13). I am calling on your name, so I know you have saved me now, you also said, ' ... that if you confess with your mouth the Lord Jesus and believe in your heart that God has raised Him from the dead, you will be saved. For with the heart one believes to righteousness, and with the mouth, confession is made to salvation" (Romans 10:9, 10).

I believe in my heart that Jesus Christ is the Son of God. I believe He was raised from the dead for my justification. And I confess Him now as my Lord; because Your Word says, "with the heart one believes to righteousness... "and I do believe with my heart, I have now become the righteousness of God in Christ (2 Corinthians. 5:21).

And I am saved! Thank you, Lord! I can now truthfully say, I see myself as a born-again, child of God!

Glory to God! Amen.

CHAPTER 4
EYE OPENING EVENT

SEVERAL YEARS PRIOR TO the "birth" of this book I shared my thoughts on this subject with my daughter's high school track coach. She agreed the issue needed addressing and that it was something the girls she coached needed to hear. She invited me to speak to the girl's track team. Amazingly they hung on my every word and were interested and intrigued by what I had to say.

To this day, the thing I remember most about the time I spent with them was the answer I received when I asked the following question: "How many of you want to be like your mothers when they grow up?"

Only two out of the forty girls raised their hands.

I asked them why they did not want to be like their mothers and their responses ranged from:

- She doesn't do anything for herself—to make herself happy, even though my dad does whatever he wants.

- She is weak.
- She doesn't have an exciting life.
- She is only a maid, caregiver, chauffeur and the cook.

They all agreed that they knew their mothers loved them. However, they did not feel their mothers demonstrated they loved themselves. The girls viewed this lack of outwardly expressing self-worth and self-respect as a weakness and as a sort of victim mentality.

A lot of times as parents we tell our children to not worry about us when they know we are sad or unhappy. We assure them their happiness makes us happy and that's what is most important—their happiness.

In doing this, we are making a conscious decision to put our family before everything else and assuming they will understand and appreciate the sacrifices we are making. Ironically, our sacrifices tend to have the exact opposite effect on our children—especially pre-teens and teenagers. Instead of appreciation and understanding, children feel resentful and distressed. They see our actions as a not-so-pleasant lesson or precursor to what they have waiting for them once they enter a relationship or marriage and become a parent. They don't see your sacrifice as a gift. They see it as a warning sign that if they end up where you're at, their happiness will be trampled underfoot; making them dependent on outside sources (like you are) to get any (happiness). The saddest part of this is that no one asked you to do this. Somehow you acquired this take one for the team attitude. But as the years progress you became resentful, because you feel undervalued and unappreciated. You did not intend for this to happen...

But, because of God's grace and the fact you are still living, you now have a chance to show yourself and your children something different. Let's give them a healthy example of ourselves that we all can be proud of. Do you want to live a fulfilling life while being happy? We shall discuss that in the next chapter.

CHAPTER 5
LIVING A FULL LIFE

EVERYONE DESIRES A FULFILLING life. No one in their right mind would give up the opportunity to be happy and fulfilled. But getting there can be a long and sometimes difficult road. There will always be trials and failures. But never let these temporary setbacks hinder you from achieving your dreams and accomplishing your goals.

Having a fulfilling life is mainly a choice. Bad, scary, and sad experiences will always be present in this life. How you choose to react and learn from these events is what counts. Getting up as quickly as possible after you fall is what counts. If you learn to do this, then your life will be brighter and better.

WAYS TO HAVE A LIFE WELL-LIVED

First and foremost, one of the key factors in the journey towards having a fulfilling life is choosing to be happy and to have joy. I know this is easier said than done, but it is the best way to have a wonderful life. Nothing is easy in life in the natural. But, remember we can rest in Christ.

"Come to me, all you who are weary and burdened, and I will give you rest. Take my yoke upon you and learn from me, for I am gentle and humble in heart, and you will find rest for your souls. For my yoke is easy and my burden is light"
(Matthew 11:28-30).

Many of us can't find happiness because of the guilt we carry or the sin we struggle with. We can't get it right by trying to keep the laws, otherwise known as the Deca Laws, which means ten, mostly known as the Ten Commandments. These are found in the Old Testament or Old Covenant in the Bible.

Wait! I want to hover right here before we go any further. If you are currently living in bondage trying to keep the laws, I want to show you what the Bible says about this.

"Sin is no longer your master, for you no longer live under the requirements of the law, Instead, you live under the freedom of God's grace"
(Romans 6:14).

If you are not delivered and shouting, I am shouting for you! Christ's death and sacrifice were the fulfillment of the laws in the Old Testament or Old Covenant. Then in the New Testament, or New Covenant, after Christ's death, God loved us so much that He gave us one of the greatest gifts, the presence of the Holy Spirit, to take residence in us forever, to show us He will never leave us or forsake us. Here's more Good News! Once you are saved you are always saved. Yes, even, when we get out of character. We are made in God's image, therefore our character is the image of God. Apologize to the person, ask for forgiveness, get up and get back to God's business which is your purpose. God wants us to have a life of abundance and happiness. Always remember to count your blessings daily no matter how small and be thankful. You may think what you are going through right now is terrible, but, I am sure if you look at the world, you will be amazed how many other situations are worse. Have a heart of thanksgiving.

"Consider it pure joy, my brothers and sisters, whenever you face trials of many kinds, because you know that the testing of your faith produces perseverance"
(James 1:2-3).

Next, it is time to let go. Let go of all those bad emotions, grudges, old habits, fears, and obsessions. All of these clutter up your life and take up space that could be used for happy and positive things. When you let these go, you free up space in your heart and mind for more wonderful possibilities. You need to let go and let more love in your life. Let go and let God! Try it! You must grab opportunities to live a fulfilling life. If you want to live your life fulfilled on purpose, you must be ready to take some risks. It may be scary but have faith and do not let old fears hold you back. Besides, I am sure you have heard that faith and fear cannot coexist in the same place.

Read the definitions of both. Do you agree?

1. Faith - complete trust or confidence in someone or something.
2. Fear - be afraid of someone or something.

Just let go of fears and expectations and trust God, so that you can be free to take steps toward your dreams and your purpose. You may have moments of failure, but the satisfaction of having tried and trusting God makes it all worth the effort. Many trials come to sharpen us and grow us and make us better.

Next, do what is important to you. It is always good to prioritize and figure out what you want to do and establish some goals. We will explore these things in greater detail later in the book. You need to work hard for the things you want. It always helps to have a sense of purpose in your life, which is a mission.

The last, but not the lesser part of having a fulfilling life, is to do what you love. Do not get lost in the black and white of life. Celebrate each second and breath you take. Feed your passions occasionally, keep doing what makes you happy, and whatever makes an impact in the lives of others.

CHAPTER 6
SUCCESS BY FULLFILLING OUR LIFE PURPOSE

WE ALL WANT TO be happy and successful in life, yet very few people can claim to be as happy and successful as they wish to be. "Why am I here?" "What do I want to do in my life?" "Where am I going?" If we do not find answers to these questions, we will continue to feel unfulfilled. The only way to achieve lasting happiness and success is by living a life of purpose. Most of the peak performers in life are those who have a vertical relationship with God and spend most of their time thinking about who they are through Him. They continuously assess their progress and consider who they are and what their calling is.

We are all unique and were put on this earth to do something extraordinary. There has never been anyone in the entire universe exactly like us. Each one of us was created with outstanding abilities, skills, talents, and gifts and make us different from all other people who have ever lived. We have the capacity within us to accomplish more than we ever imagined possible.

Each one of us is born with a unique life purpose, and our mission is to discover the key role we are meant to fill and then to throw our whole heart into doing it exceptionally well. Plato once said, "This is a place that you are to fill and no one else can fill, something you are to do, which no one else does." We can achieve greater success and happiness and have deeper fulfillment by finding and living our purpose.

"I pray that the eyes of your heart may be enlightened in order that you may know the hope to which he has called you, the riches of his glorious inheritance in his holy people, and his incomparably great power for us who believe. That power is the same as the mighty strength"
(Ephesians 1:18-19 NIV) .

DO YOU KNOW YOUR PURPOSE?

Most people today do not know their purpose, and they wander around aimlessly and accomplish very little in life. They respond to circumstances, situation and events, to parents, responsibilities, and relationships and never take the time to sit down and think about what it is that they want for themselves. They spend their entire life doing things they do not enjoy, and they work only to earn a living and to pay their bills. As Thoreau rightly said, "The mass of men lead lives of quiet desperation." These people achieve only temporary success and happiness because they set and achieve only short-term goals. Once these goals are achieved, they still feel something is missing in their lives and they are unfulfilled. Most high achievers in life think and act differently. They believe in a mission which goes far beyond a simple goal. These people are committed to following their purpose and do only those things they enjoy most, and which give meaning to their lives.

To find our true calling, we need to understand ourselves better and know exactly what we enjoy doing the most in life.

We can begin to ask ourselves questions like:

What activities are most important to you?

_____

What do you have the most fun doing?

_____

What do you do that you lose track of time?

_____

What would you do if you had no limitations?

_____

What would you do if you knew you could not fail?

_____

What are the things you do best in life?

_____

What would you do for free for the rest of your life if you had all the money you needed?

_____

What do others look to you for?

_____

What do people closest to you say your passions are?

_____

We must dare to take a risk and go against the norm if we want to discover and fulfill our life purpose. We must be willing to do what our hearts desire and follow our bliss rather than follow what other people want us to do. Following our heart and the Holy Spirit rather than following the crowd gives us a better chance to find happiness and fulfillment, but it takes courage and guts. Many people are afraid of being different, of not being accepted by those around them and of standing out rather than blending in. We must always listen to the wise words of Oprah Winfrey who once said, "I was once afraid of people saying, 'Who does she think she is?' Now I have the courage to stand and say, 'This is who I am.'"

Our truth is ours to live, and no apology is necessary. Once we begin to live our life on purpose, we will become more passionate about what we are doing and become so involved in our task we will lose track of time. For us, work will become play because we enjoy every moment and spend our time doing what we love and what we are meant to do. Confucius was right when he said, "Find a job you love, and you'll never work a day in your life."

Furthermore, when we live our purpose, things will seem to fall into place. The people, opportunities, and resources we need come to us easily and effortlessly. Joseph Campbell once said "If you follow your bliss you put yourself on a kind of track that has been there all the while, waiting for you, and the life that you ought to be living is the one you are living. When you can see that, you begin to meet people who are in your field of bliss, and they open doors to you. I say, follow your bliss and don't be afraid, and doors will open where you didn't know they were going to be."

The whole world will also benefit because when we are in alignment with our true calling, all our actions will automatically serve others and we will make a difference in the lives of others by giving value to them far beyond what we could imagine.

A purpose driven life is a life we must all seek to live. Identifying and honoring our purpose is the key to success and happiness in life. We can become everything God wants us to become while living a life of purpose and fulfilling our highest natural potential. This is the greatest and most precious gift we can give to ourselves and the world. Deepak Chopra was right when he said "Everyone has a purpose in life … a unique gift or special talent to give to others. And when we blend this unique talent with service to others, we experience the ecstasy and exultation of our own spirit, which is the ultimate goal of all goals."

This aligns with God's will for our lives, so He will, in turn, receive all the glory. Congratulations you have begun to Uncover your Original Blueprint. Now that you are transitioning towards your purpose let's explore the 10 Steps that will help you re-discover the real you and help you continue your journey back to you.

PART 2: 10 STEPS TO YOUR REBIRTH

In this section, you will find guidance and encouragement to roll up your sleeves and get to the root of what it will take to move in a positive and productive direction. By following these steps, there is a better chance you will experience life with fulfillment and joy the way you were meant to experience it. I am excited for you!

CHAPTER 7

STEP 1: TACKLING THE EPIDEMIC

SIMPLY PUT, TACKLING THE problem happens when your truth sets you free.

Remember how I mentioned earlier that part of the healing process and one of the keys to getting back on track is acknowledging and understanding the role you played in getting yourself lost? Do you remember the list of things you did to get to where you are? We're going to revisit that list. This time, I want you to circle the items that describe you that made you a victim of circumstances.

- For the sake of not putting the relationship at risk, you did not provide honest feedback expressing your true feelings, likes, and dislikes in the early stages of the relationship. It worked, so you maintained the status quo to keep the relationship going.
- You gave up your job for the good of the family; making you feel as though you had lost leverage

in the relationship. Doing so also made you devalue your self-worth and led you to reclassify yourself as a dependent.

- You allowed your mate to assume the parent role over you and you responded in obedience.
- You allowed someone to carve you into what they wanted you to be or fix you even though you were not broken.
- You traded in your dreams and aspirations for someone else's.
- You were too accessible and did not bring your own life or existence into the relationship.
- You wanted the relationship so badly you were willing to do whatever it took to make it work, even if it meant compromising your own values.
- You had not defined who you were prior to the relationship, so you did not have anything to hold on to.
- You forgot you only have one life to live.
- You forgot you already had a purpose in life long before you took on titles like Wife/Husband, Doctor, Teacher, and Mother/Father.
- You may have been tempted or lured by material security.
- You stopped doing some of the things you enjoyed before or during the early stages of the relationship (going to church, hobbies spending time with family and friends.) so your mate did not know this was part of who you used to be.

When I completed this list, there were more things that described me than I wanted to admit. Amazedly, it is neither a trick nor coincidence that most of the things on the list start with the word "YOU." This was sobering and painful for me to see and accept about myself. I blamed others, became disappointed, and thought:

- "How could I have allowed this to happen to me?"
- "Maybe I deserved it because I did not value my self-worth and stand up for myself."
- "Why was I willing to sacrifice myself for a relationship?"
- "How could I have been so blind?"
- "How could I have convinced myself that a shopping trip in the beginning, was so thoughtful and not see it as possibly the start of being molded into what he wanted to see me in and that my current style was being replaced?"

You are probably thinking I went way too far on that last thought, and maybe that was not the intent. But, to me, time seemed to confirm this thought to some degree. No matter what I pulled out to wear, I always heard, "Are you wearing that? What about this?" Even when I was already dressed—which should have been evident I had already made my selection and my choice. I hope you realize the problem wasn't him asking me these questions. The problem was how I complied. I gave in to his wishes—even if I was already dressed.

Unfortunately, this was not the saddest part of this situation. The most detrimental aspect of this whole situation was the effect it had on our daughter. When she got old enough to feel like she could talk to me about it, she told me how frustrated and angry it made her when her dad did this to me. I could have used that to my advantage in garnering sympathy, but I didn't. That would have been both wrong and deceitful. I had to explain to her that he did not make me change. I did it on my own. I gave up my power even though I did not realize that was what I was doing. I encouraged my daughter to not compromise her choices for anyone. Because I'm writing this book, it's probably not hard for you to guess that I'm no longer letting anyone choose my wardrobe these days. One day I decided that was going to stop. I was a grown woman capable of choosing my wardrobe. After all, hadn't I attracted him without his help in picking out my clothes? Surely my decision to dress myself, would not have been a deal-breaker for our relationship. Our relationship was stronger than that. It's sad I did not think about it this way.

If you've never been in this type of position, you're lucky, because unfortunately, it is a lot more common than you think. It's a common problem because it has been happening for generations without anyone thinking twice about it. It is the position many of our grandparents, mothers, and fathers have taken in their relationships for years.

But the excuse of "we've always done it that way" doesn't make something right. Let's get down to the business of addressing this and the other warning signs from that list and help you turn things around. Then you can enjoy and experience life in a full measure that will only serve to enhance the joy and happiness there is to be had in your relationships, and restore confidence in yourself.

CHAPTER 8

STEP 2: HOW YOU GOT HERE

WHAT A JOURNEY IT has been to reach this point in our lives! The most significant question we usually ask ourselves is, "How did we get here?" Time seems to pass so quickly that often we cannot even recall what we've done or the places we've been. Here is one thing you can bank on: We were created for a purpose. Psalm 139:15-16 (NIV) states, "My frame was not hidden from you when I was made in the secret place when I was woven together in the depths of the earth. Your eyes saw my unformed body; all the days ordained for me were written in your book before one of them came to be." Other Scriptures that point to this truth include:

"He has told you, O man, what is good; and what does the Lord require of you but to do justice, and to love kindness, and to walk humbly with your God?" (Micah 6:8 ESV).

"The Lord will fulfill his purpose for me; your steadfast love, O Lord, endures forever. Do not forsake the work of your hands"
(Psalm 138:8 ESV).

"For I know the plans I have for you," declares the Lord, "plans to prosper you and not to harm you, plans to give you hope and a future"
(Jeremiah 29:11 NIV).

"Agree with God and be at peace; thereby good will come to you"
(Job 22:21 ESV).

"Or do you not know that your body is a temple of the Holy Spirit within you, whom you have from God? You are not your own, for you were bought with a price. So, glorify God in your body"
(1 Corinthians 6:19-20 ESV).

The truth of the matter, however, is that most of us are still trying to discover precisely what that purpose is. We feel like we're in a race we must finish, but we aren't sure where we're racing to or how long the race will be. People in their twenties and early thirties see it as an exciting challenge and something to look forward to. But once you get past your mid-thirties, anxiety sets in, to some extent, because you aren't sure you have what it takes to finish, and/or you don't know if you are on the right track. Another problem in running this race comes when you listen to the wrong cheering section. If you are listening to what society has deemed important to race toward then you are most likely passing up what is important in life and going for the temporal instead of what matters most—the things that ensure the spiritual and emotional well-being and create solid bonds. This is where the saying "stop to smell the roses," comes into play.

Sadly, not many of us are doing this. Instead, we are so focused on what lies ahead we miss the little things that help us connect the dots of our existence. Is that what has happened to you? If your answer is "yes," the next question you need to ask yourself is, "Why am I rushing through life?"

That happened to me, and I did not realize I had put myself on a hamster's wheel. I think part of the reason was wanting to advance past my current situations. I didn't realize the precious tools and lessons God had for me in those seasons. You have heard many times that God gives you what you need.

If we understand this Scripture we know having faith and believing in God is a test and He has it all under control. All we need is faith. Matthew 17:20 (NLT) says, "I tell you the truth, if you have faith as small as a mustard seed, you can say to this mountain, 'Move from here to here' and it will move. Nothing would be impossible." Slow down, smell those roses, and sometimes just be still.

STILL

Still is when I see my chest rise and fall as I hear my own breath move from my lungs through the atmosphere forcefully like seeds from a blown dandelion.
Still is when I look around and see a mirror, only it is not a mirror on the wall, but a mirror to my soul.
Sill is when I smell a bittersweet scent moving past my nose, and my eyes then scan each corner of the room to see what is omitting such a scent, only to realize it is my disposition.
Still is when you dare to dream while you're awake and smile in your sleep, only to be awakened by your own movement as you adjust yourself to achieve comfort again in your own familiar space.
Still is when you feel a faint brush against your skin that brings chill bumps to its surface like the stirring of your spirit.
Still is good sometimes.

—Sonyia Graham

Often, we see or experience things we don't like or agree with and instead of voicing our feelings or concerns we close our eyes and ears. We act as though these things will disappear, or like we are fooling someone else when we are mainly fooling ourselves. Any of these scenarios could have aided in placing ourselves in this position:

- For the sake of the relationship, you did not give feedback expressing your true interest and dislikes at the beginning of the relationship.
- Maybe you gave up your job to take care of the

family, and lost leverage and self-worth and were reclassified as a dependent.

- You allowed your mate to assume the parent role over you and you responded in obedience.
- You allowed someone to carve you into what they wanted you to be or fix you even though you were not broken.
- You traded in your dreams and aspirations for someone else's.
- You were too accessible and did not bring your own life or existence into the relationship.
- You wanted the relationship so badly you were willing to do whatever it took to make it work, even if it meant compromising your own value or values.
- You had not defined who you were, so you did not have a model to hold on to.
- You forgot you only have one life to live and that it was yours.
- You forgot you already had a purpose in life long before you took on titles like Wife/Husband, Doctor and Mother/Father.
- You may have even been persuaded by material security
- You stopped doing some of the things you enjoyed before the relationship (going to church, hobbies spending time with family and friends).

The good news is, once you acknowledge, understand, and accept the role you played and how you got to this place, you are moving in the right direction. The next step will be to remind yourself of what happiness is and how to achieve it.

CHAPTER 9

STEP 3: WHAT IS HAPPINESS?

ONE DICTIONARY DEFINES HAPPINESS as the state of being happy; a feeling of glee, delight, contentment, satisfaction, and joy.

Sounds great, doesn't it? Aren't we all looking for happiness? In America, happiness is viewed as a fundamental right. What do we know about happiness? Are we born with it? Can we make ourselves happier? Why does something make one person happy but not another? Why is it easy for some people to be happy? Researchers are learning more about the answers to these questions—and that's great. But that research isn't doing much to help you now, so ask yourself: What would it take to make YOU happy? Do you know, or are you focused on the happiness of others to the extent you cannot see beyond their happiness to your own?

WHAT DOES HAPPINESS MEAN TO YOU?

Let's take another look at the definition of happiness: the state of being happy; a feeling of glee, delight, contentment, satisfaction, and joy. Psychologist Ed Diener, author of *Happiness: Unlocking the Mysteries of Psychological Wealth*, defines happiness in more technical terms. He defines it in terms of what psychologists call "subjective well-being," which is a combination of life-satisfaction and having more positive emotions than negative emotions.

Martin Seligman, the author of *Authentic Happiness*, describes happiness as having three parts: pleasure, engagement, and meaning. Pleasure is the feel-good part of happiness. Engagement refers to living a good life of work, family, friends, and hobbies. Meaning refers to using our strengths to contribute to a larger purpose. Seligman says all three are important, but of the three, engagement and meaning make the most difference to living a happy life.

Several synonyms can be used to define happiness, but that's nothing compared to the number of ways people can achieve happiness — so many ways, in fact, that for many, happiness appears to be elusive … out of reach. We want to be happy, and we can say whether we are or not, but is there a way to study and measure the effects of happiness? And if so, might we be able to use what we learn to become even happier? Psychologists say yes and that there are good reasons for doing so. They call it "Positive Psychology."

POSITIVE PSYCHOLOGY

Positive Psychology is "the scientific study of the strengths and virtues that enable individuals and communities to thrive." The research involved includes studying strengths, positive emotions, and resilience in relation to a person's proclaimed level of happiness. They base the validity of their research on the claim that by studying only psychological disorders gives us only part of the picture of mental health.

But by studying levels of happiness and mental wellness, we can learn new ways to recover from or prevent anxiety, depression and other psychological disorders.

HAPPINESS VS JOY

Up to this point, I've used the word "happy" to describe the state of being you should be striving to achieve for yourself. And for the most part, I will continue to do that because this is the word we most readily associate with our discussion. Semantically speaking, however, the word we should be using is "joy."

Technically speaking the word "happy" indicates fulfillment or satisfaction derived from an outside source. For example, shopping for a new dress makes some people happy, while spending the day fishing or water skiing makes other people happy

Joy, however, is something that comes from the inside. It doesn't depend on events, circumstances, people or things. It is a state of mind. You decide to be joyous in spite of what is going on around you. The Bible speaks of joy and happiness this way:

Joy

"But the fruit of the Spirit is love, joy, peace, forbearance, kindness, goodness, faithfulness, gentleness, and self-control"
(Galatians 5:22-23 NIV).

There is no mention of happiness in the fruit of the Spirit because the Spirit is within us. Joy, along with the other elements of the fruit of the Spirit are states of being … mindsets rather than controlled situations.

"A joyful heart is good medicine, but a crushed spirit dries up the bones"
(Proverbs 17:22 ESV).

Have you ever thought about the fact that we can be "brain dead" but we cannot be "heart dead"? Our bodies can still have life in them even after our minds cease to function, but if the heart stops, life does, too. Therefore, it behooves us to fill our hearts with joy so that our minds and spirits will remain healthy and strong no matter what is going on around us.

"Count it all joy, my brothers, when you meet trials of
various kinds, for you know that the testing of your
faith produces steadfastness. And let steadfastness
have its full effect, that you may be perfect and
complete, lacking in nothing"
(James 1:2-4 ESV).

Nowhere do you see in these verses anything about
being happy when bad things happen. That would be
mean—heartless, even. It would also be completely
against human nature. But when we have joy, which is
the knowledge that what is taking place on the outside
of our lives cannot extinguish the hope and comfort we
have in Jesus, we can be unhappy (sad), without that
unhappiness taking control of our thoughts and actions.
It is a feeling that can be soothed and eased over time
and by clinging to faith in the promises of Jesus, which
results in … joy.

"A woman giving birth to a child has pain because her
time has come, but when her baby is born she forgets
the anguish because of her joy that a child is born into
the world. So, with you: Now is your time of grief,
but I will see you again and you will rejoice, and no
one will take away your joy"
(John 16:21-22 NIV).

And yet another indicator is joy doesn't depend on something or someone, which means it cannot be taken away from you. You and only you have the power to have … keep … lose … or refuse joy.

"For the kingdom of God is not a matter of eating and drinking, but of righteousness, peace and joy in the Holy Spirit…"
(Romans 14:17 NIV).

The preceding Scripture is by far my favorite verse about joy. It is also the most definitive. This verse clearly and indisputably puts the truth about joy out there. No one can find joy in anyone or anything other than the Holy Spirit, which is Jesus' presence post-death, burial, resurrection, and ascension.

Now let's look at what the Bible has to say about happiness and how it compares to joy …

Happiness

"Then Leah said, "How happy I am! The women will call me happy." So, she named him Asher"
(Genesis 30:13 NIV).

As you can plainly see, Leah's happiness stemmed from the circumstance of becoming a mother. If you know her full story (found in Genesis chapters 29-36) you understand why this was important to her—why her happiness was wrapped up in things and people ... and how that happiness came and went throughout her lifetime. Happiness is the same for all of us when it is tied to something or someone else.

"Haman went out that day happy and in high spirits. But when he saw Mordecai at the king's gate and observed that he neither rose nor showed fear in his presence, he was filled with rage against Mordecai" (Esther 5:9 NIV).

Haman's happiness stemmed from his evil desires. Sin often causes us to be happy, too. How sad, this statement is, but the truth it holds should make us even more mindful of the difference between joy and happiness and why we should take such care to differentiate between the two.

"But may the righteous be glad and rejoice before God; may they be happy and joyful" (Psalm 68: 3 NIV).

The thing you need to notice in this verse is the fact that David deliberately lists them as two things: being happy and being joyful.

"A happy heart makes the face cheerful, but heartache crushes the spirit"
(Proverbs 15:13 NIV).

This verse is similar in nature to Proverbs 17:22. The difference I want to point out, though, is this: a happy heart makes the face cheerful, but in the other verse, joy is medicine for the spirit. This verse looks at the condition of the heart from the outside in, whereas the previous verse looks at the condition of the heart from the inside out.

"When times are good, be happy; but when times are bad, consider this: God has made the one as well as the other ..."
(Ecclesiastes 7:14a: NIV).

And finally, Solomon writes in Ecclesiastes that times, i.e. things, people, events, etc., are what make us happy. He says we will experience both happiness and sadness, but God is present in both of those times. His presence should sustain us.

So, which is right? Have I been wrong to this point in this book by telling you to pursue your own happiness? Should I have been using the word joy instead? Yes and No.

- Yes, when looking at it from the perspective of inner satisfaction and fulfillment.
- No, when you consider the fact that the two are commonly interchanged; meaning you relate easier to the word happy than you do the word joy. In using the words happy and happiness you are quicker to identify with what I'm saying and how it applies to your situation.
- And no, because several of the things we've talked about so far, are based on you doing something to give you happiness ... and joy.

From this point on, however, I do want you to be more aware of the differences between joy and happiness even though the word happiness (or some form of it) is what you will see. Got it? Great, then let's continue by looking at the habits of happy people and how you can become habitually happy (joyful), too.

ARE YOU HAPPY?

I want you to take the Happiness Quiz. Circle the answer that best fits you.

1. Are your ideas and spiritual beliefs reflected in your goals and your life?

   Yes, I regularly set goals and try to focus and live my life on my terms.

   No, I get through my days with little thought or strategy of what I want or what I believe.

2. Do you make regular ME Time for yourself?
   Yes, I get away from it all when I can even if it is not as often as I would like.

   No, I am always rushed and worn out. Finding time for me is not an option.

3. Do you have supportive friends you can rely on?

   Yes, I know no matter what, I have supportive friends there to support me or bail me out, no questions asked.

   No, I have friends, but the friendship is more superficial. I do share my problems with them, but I'm not sure I could count on them if I did.

4. Do you like what you do?

   Yes, For the most part, I enjoy what I do.

   No, I am stressed out on a regular basis, but I do it because I don't know what else to do.

5. Is there romance in your relationship?

   Yes, we enjoy one another, and it shows in the way we talk, play, and interact.

   No. We are more like friends with benefits instead of a couple in love. Much of our relationship is just going through the motions.

6. Are you at ease with your financial situation?

   Yes, by living within my means I have taken most of the stress out of my financial life. It could always be better, but I do not feel under constant stress.

   No, I am struggling and stressing on a regular basis.

7. Are you learning something new or improving your skills or knowledge base on a regular basis?

   Yes, I try to learn something new on a regular basis. Small personal development helps me to feel good about myself and stay on top of my game.

   No, Not very often. I focus on getting things done the best way I know and don't take much time to learn something new.

8. Is your health a priority?

   Yes, I am not perfect, but I do think about my health and try to make wise choices when it comes to eating and exercise.

   No, Health is an afterthought and usually only gets my attention when I am not feeling well.

9. Do you have a strong sense of self-worth?

   Yes, I believe in myself. I am happy with who I am.

   No, I doubt myself often, and regularly compare myself and focus on ways I do not measure up to others.

10. Are you part of a peer group, club, or church that give you a sense of community?

    Yes, I am part of at least one that I enjoy and look forward to meeting with them. The group gives me a sense of belonging.

    No, I don't have a group that I feel connected to or gives me a sense of belonging.

11. Are you satisfied with your relationship with your family?

    Yes, we are not perfect, but I know that we love one another, and they are there for me when I need them.

    No, most of my family relationships cause me stress, and I cannot count on them for support or encouragement.

12. Are you still dreaming and looking forward to what the future holds?

Yes, I have dreams and goals and they make me smile as I think of them.

No, I have not thought about what I want in a long time. For the most part, my focus is usually on the day to day or other's needs and wants.

Add up how many Yes questions you circled. Answers to your results are as follows:

9-12 Your score suggests you are mostly happy with your life. Everything may not be perfect, but chances are you would not change most things if given the chance. Keep following your sense of purpose to experience your fullest life possible. A positive outlook will help you stay on course to continue achieving your dreams and goals.

7-8 Your score suggests there are parts of your life that you are happy with, but there may be some areas you would change or hope to improve if you had the chance. Joy may be found by simplifying your life. Work on enjoying a few meaningful things instead of doing too many less meaningful ones. Recognize that there is a difference between chasing after happiness and choosing happiness. Slow down, appreciate and observe what is in you and around you.

4-6 Your score suggests there are some areas in your life in which you could be happier. You can start your Re-discovery process to uncover your dreams and wants and to become more aware of how you may be limiting your own happiness. Decide on what is important and focus in on those areas.

0-3 Your score suggests you are not happy as you could be right now. It could be because of something that happened recently, or you have had a bad day. Whatever the case, take a good look at why you feel the way you do. Small changes can make a big difference. Remember it's not someone else's job to make you happy. Get help and support to help you through tough times.

THE 7 HABITS OF HAPPY PEOPLE

1. **Express your heart.** People who have one or more close friendships are happier. It doesn't seem to matter if we have a large network of close relationships or not. What seems to make a difference is if and how often we cooperate in activities and share our personal feelings with a friend or relative

2. **Caring -** Cultivate kindness. People who volunteer or simply care for others on a consistent basis seem to be happier and less depressed. Although "caring" can involve volunteering as part of an organized group or club, it can be as simple as reaching out to a colleague or classmate who looks lonely or is struggling with an issue.

3. **Exercise -** Keep moving. Regular exercise is associated with improved mental well-being and a lower incidence of depression. The

Cochrane Review (the most influential medical review of its kind in the world) has produced a landmark analysis of 23 studies on exercise and depression. One of the major conclusions was that exercise had a "large clinical impact."

4. **Flow** - Find your flow. If we are deeply involved in trying to reach a goal or an activity that is challenging but well suited to our skills, we experience a joyful state called "flow."

5. **Spiritual Engagement and Meaning -** Discovering Meaning. Studies demonstrate a close link between spiritual and religious practice and happiness. Spirituality is closely related to the discovery of greater meaning in our lives. As the psychologist Martin Seligman emphasizes, through the meaningful life we discover a deeper kind of happiness,

6. **Strengths and Virtues -** Discover and use your strengths. Studies by experts such as Martin Seligman in the new field of Positive Psychology show that the happiest people are those that have discovered their unique strengths (such as persistence and critical thinking) and virtues (such as humanity). They use those strengths and virtues for a purpose that is greater than their own personal goals (Authentic Happiness: Using the New Positive Psychology to Realize Your Potential for Lasting Fulfillment).

7. **Positive Mindset: Optimism, Mindfulness and Gratitude -** Treasure gratitude, mindfulness, and hope. Of all the areas studied in the relatively young field of positive

psychology, gratitude has perhaps received the most attention. According to studies conducted by Martin Seligman, grateful people have been shown to have greater positive emotion, a greater sense of belonging, and lower incidence of depression and stress.

For more on this topic visit the Pursuit of Happiness organization's website at www.pursuit-of-happiness. org.

CHAPTER 10
STEP 4: SELF-ESTEEM

SOME PEOPLE BELIEVE self-esteem is something that is given and shown. Maybe when you were growing up, your mother said you were pretty/handsome, your father said you were smart, and you always receive compliments from others. Many people who did not experience this at an early age, use this as an excuse for their lack of self-esteem. It is important that parents let their children know the positive aspects they see in them as they nurture and give them encouragement. The truth is, self-esteem does not come from the exterior or from what others see in you. It is completely the opposite — that's why it starts with the word self.

"If you want to Soar in Life you must first Learn to
F.L.Y
(First Love Yourself)"
—**Mark Sterling**

Definition of SELF-ESTEEM

Confidence and satisfaction in oneself: self-respect

"There are three (3) factors that were identified that uniquely contribute to people's global self-esteem: (a) people's tendencies to experience positive and negative affective states, (b) people's specific self-views (i.e., their conceptions of their strengths and weaknesses), and (c) the way people frame their self-views. Framing factors included the relative certainty and importance of people's positive versus negative self-views and the discrepancy between people's actual and ideal self-views. The contribution of importance to people's self-esteem, however, was qualified in 2 ways. First, importance contributed only to the self-esteem of those who perceived that they had relatively few talents. Second, individuals who saw their positive self-views as important were especially likely to be high in self-esteem when they were also highly certain of these positive self-views. The theoretical and therapeutic implications of these findings are discussed." (PsycINFO Database Record (c) 2012
— APA ©2015 American Psychological Association

"As long as the mind is enslaved, the body can never be free. Psychological freedom, a firm sense of self-esteem, is the most powerful weapon against the long night of physical slavery..."
"Be an artist at whatever you do. Even if you are a street sweeper, be the Michelangelo of street sweepers ..."
"Each of us is something of a schizophrenic personality, tragically divided against ourselves ..."
—Dr. Martin Luther King Jr.

So, what is our self-worth according to the Bible?

"So God made mankind in his own image, in the image of God he created them; male and female he created them"
(Genesis 1:27 NIV).

"And we all, who with unveiled faces contemplate the Lord's glory, are being transformed into his image with ever-increasing glory, which comes from the Lord, who is the Spirit"
(2 Corinthians 3:18).

"For you created my inmost being; you knit me together in my mother's womb. I praise you because I am fearfully and wonderfully made; your works are wonderful, I know that full well"
(Psalm 139:13-14 NIV).

The most important part is to believe in yourself which is easier said than done. We have so many demands on us that it is often difficult to feel that we are at our best at any of them.

Do any of these sound familiar? Your clothes fit a little tighter than you would like, and your skin could be a little firmer; your teenager just argued with you and stormed out of the room; the new manager at work is changing procedures and delegating work so fast that it is making your head spin. Well, take a deep breath and relax. To improve your outlook and boost your self-esteem, you need to focus on the good and positive instead of the negative in your day and life. Check out these simple steps that can help you to believe in yourself.

1. Make a list of the things you like about yourself and be sure to refer to it often. It is hard to remember your strengths when the day is going downhill fast. Read your list often and remember these points during the day when things get challenging.

2. Learn to accept and believe compliments. Try not to deflect them but accept them and believe them. Add them to your list of positives. If you keep hearing these compliments, they must be true. Just say, "Thank you."

3. Take the time to do and enjoy something where you excel. When you do something you're good at you get a sense of accomplishment that will help you to feel good about yourself.

4. And finally, always remember to take the time to relax and find quiet time for yourself. Take a bubble bath, get a massage, watch a movie that makes you laugh and smile, enjoy yoga, meditate or do whatever you enjoy. Take the time to refocus your mind on your strengths and positives so you can be strong and believe in yourself.

1. What do I like about myself?

_____

_____

_____

_____

_____

2. What are my strengths?

_____

_____

_____

_____

_____

"Do not conform to the pattern of this world, but be transformed by the renewing of your mind. Then you will be able to test and approve what God's will is— his good, pleasing and perfect will" (Romans 12:2 NIV).

Remember how I mentioned that hearing compliments about yourself makes you feel good? Well, who said you must wait for them to come from someone else? You might have heard if you do something for 21 days it becomes a habit. Recite these affirmations or write some of your own and begin to renew your mind daily and reprogram it with positive, powerful self-worth statements that reinforce self-love and respect for yourself.

21 DAILY SELF ESTEEM AFFIRMATIONS

These are designed to replace your inner voice of self-defeat while building feelings of self-worth.

1. Today, I will exemplify greatness by being the best me, I can be.

2. My life is important—many people love and respect me, and I, them.

3. I have the power to determine my day.

4. My smile is infectious, and it will be a blessing to someone, today.

5. I am unique and wonderfully made.

6. My mind is keen and resourceful, and that allows me to perceive solutions or problems that may arise, and solve them.

7. Every breath I take is filled with the peace that resides in me.

8. I am a good person and I deserve to have good things, as well as, joy.

9. I am intelligent and innovative.

10. My body is healthy and strong inside out.

11. My mind is sharp and I grow wiser each day.

12. I give out love and care, and I accept love and care from others.

13. I do not live in the past because I have a great expectation for today.

14. I embrace people for the way they are so they will embrace me as I am.

15. I possess a heart of thanksgiving for even the little things.

16. This is my life and I am free to determine my life's direction and choices.

17. I am filled with love, kindness, and laughter.

18. My presence creates an atmosphere of positivity so that people love to be around me.

19. When people see me, they can't help but see and feel the presence of God.

20. I am well-versed in many areas, yet I am humble.

21. My flaws make me human, but, God loves me, flaws and all.

SELF ESTEEM JOURNALING

Self-esteem journaling is a powerful tool that will teach you to celebrate and give yourself credit for all of your accomplishment and victories, no matter how small. It will visually show you how amazing you are. We tend to take most of the things we do daily for granted. We sweep it under the carpet and sum it up as something we do or did and give it no value. Wow, no wonder we see no value, we are not adding any of it up.

"Everything that happens to you is a reflection of what you believe about yourself. We cannot outperform our level of self-esteem. We cannot draw to ourselves more than we think we are."
—Iyanla Vansant

Start your self-esteem journaling today. Here are 10 statements you can use in your daily self-esteem journaling.

Something I did well today …

1. Today I had fun when …
2. I felt proud when …
3. Today I accomplished …
4. I had a positive experience with (a person, place, or thing) …
5. Something I did for someone …

6. I felt good about myself when …
7. I was proud of someone else …
8. Today was interesting because …
9. A positive thing I witnessed …

Here are examples of what your self-esteem journal could resemble.

Monday
Today I had fun when I learned to play tennis.

I felt proud when I realized I had worked out five days this week.

Today I accomplished all but one task on my list today.

Tuesday
Today I took time out my day to help a friend in need.

I drank more than one glass of water today.

Continue for each day of the week.

CHAPTER 11

STEP 5: REDISCOVER YOURSELF

WHO ARE YOU?

If you removed all your titles Mother/Father, Wife/
Husband, Grandmother/Grandfather, Daughter/Son,
Granddaughter/Grandson Sister/Brother, Aunt/Uncle,
Cousin, Friend, Dr., Attorney, Pastor, or Teacher.

Who are you?

_____

_____

(Fill in the blanks)

Is your statement above a reflection of your Original
Blueprint? Is it your core DNA? I suspect it's not.

_____

_____

"Me, I would like to reintroduce you to yourself"
—Sonyia Graham

How many times a day do we walk by a mirror and not really see ourselves? What we choose to see is a shell of who we have become. For me. I believe it made it easier to look at myself. I knew if I looked at myself, it would be like unpacking a bag. A bag of possible regrets, disappointments, fear, weakness and hurt. But the saddest thing I found once I unpacked that bag was an intelligent little girl with dreams, hopes, and aspirations to change the world, that I let down and did not give a fighting chance.

In this chapter, you will be pulling back the covers on who you see in the mirror and rediscovering the parts of you that no longer are visible, by first revisiting and getting reacquainted with who you are and what makes you tick. While on this journey to remember, there may be some dark areas that bring you pain when you revisit them. Keep moving through those times. Do not relive them or get stuck there. Some of these things you will need to recall the lessons you learned, continuing moving forward and rejoicing in how far you may have already come.

"Be strong and courageous. Do not be terrified; do not be discouraged, for the Lord your God will be with you wherever you go" (Joshua 1:9).

"My past has not defined me, destroyed me, deterred me, or defeated me; it has only strengthened me."
—Steve Maraboli

Here are some things about me.

In this section, you will list the things that immediately come to mind. Do not be discouraged, if you do not have answers to all of the questions now. By the time you dive into the next part of this chapter you will be able to come back and fill in a lot of the blanks.

List the things you enjoyed in the past:

1. _____

2. _____

3. _____

4. _____

5. _____

List the things you enjoy now:

1. _____

2. _____

3. _____

4. _____

5. _____

List the things you are good at:

1. _____

2. _____

3. _____

4. _____

5. _____

List positive things people often say about you:

1. _____

2. _____

3. _____

Name travel designations you want to visit:

1. _____

2. _____

3. _____

4. _____

5. _____

Name talents or gifts you have:

1. _____

2. _____

3. _____

List what is important to you in a relationship:

1. _____

2. _____

3. _____

4. _____

5. _____

List your strengths:

1. _____

2. _____

3. _____

List your weaknesses:

1. _____

2. _____

3. _____

CHAPTER 12
STEP 6: LIFE JOURNALING IS POWERFUL

WHILE A DIARY IS a record of daily events, a Life Journal is that and much more. A diary focuses on the external aspects of your daily events, and a journal concentrates on the inner you as you experience life. In a Life Journal, you record not only what happened on a given day, but you record your emotions, understandings, thoughts, and ideas.

A LIFE JOURNAL

A Life Journal is a place where you can release your feelings and most inner thoughts without fear of judgment or blame allowing you to record insights you may be afraid to voice out loud. It is a place where you can come back to find a deeper understanding as you see an overview of your inner self and happenings in your life. There are endless benefits to journaling. Life Journal writing can lead to ideas and solutions to current problems or to an opportunity to "let go" of past experiences and events so that you can move on in life. Life Journaling can help you achieve greater personal and professional awareness, empowerment, and it can be an instrument in goal setting and actualizing personal and professional dreams. As I was considering journaling, I found Steve Pavlina's website where he talks about three powerful benefits of journal writing. Here is his list.

- **Solve tricky problems:** Some problems are difficult to solve when you're stuck in an associative, first-person viewpoint. Only when you record the situation and then re-examine it from a third-person perspective does the solution become clear. Sometimes the solution is so obvious you're shocked you didn't see it sooner.

- **Gain clarity:** A great time to turn to your journal is when you're not clear about what to do. Should you quit your job to start your own business? Should you marry your current romantic partner? Are you on the right track financially? It's amazing how much clearer things become when you explore them in writing.

- **Verify your progress:** It's wonderful to go back and re-read journal entries from years ago and see how much real progress you have achieved. When you're frustrated that your life doesn't seem to be working out as you'd like, go back and read something you wrote five years ago - it will totally change your perspective. Doing this helps you in the present moment too by reminding you,

you are in fact growing, even when it feels like you're standing still.

A Life Journal is a tool that will help you keep a record of your thoughts and emotions just as a photo album keeps track of events and occasions. Start a Life Journal today to help discover the inner you.

GETTING STARTED

WHAT YOU NEED

Journal writing can be recorded in an old spiral, fancy hardback book, or in an electronic file. Choose a journal that is usable for you. Suitable for you could mean a thin spiral that you can keep in your briefcase or small hardbound book you will keep in your bag. Make it special enough to signify its importance. Make it attractive to you so that you are drawn to it.

MAKE TIME

Finding time to journal may be one of your biggest challenges. Some people like to journal first thing in the morning to get their day focused while others prefer to journal at night to record their thoughts and feelings of the day. Find a time and a quiet place that works for you. An uninterrupted 20 to 30 minutes is ideal, but if you can only find five minutes during a break, then that will work as well. Journaling can be done daily or only several times a month. Journaling should not be a burden but a way to decompress and find your inner self. Journaling at least three to four times a week will help you get an accurate picture of what is going on in your life.

WHAT TO DO

There are no hard and fast rules on how to set up a journal. You can be as informal as you like or even record lists or draw pictures or write letters to yourself or others. It is up to you how you record your thoughts. The only must is to record a date for each entry so that you can have a reference point of when your thoughts and ideas came about. You can also record the time and place if you so desire. Remember, great writing skills are not needed when keeping a journal.

GET STARTED AND KEEP IT SAFE

Be sure to keep your journal safe and private so that you will freely record your thoughts and emotions. If your journal is available to others, you may censor your writing and not get the full benefit that journaling has to offer.

If you are having a hard time getting started, here are some prompts to help you out. Write about your dreams; childhood memories and feelings; where you would like to be in two to three years; why you wanted a journal; when do you feel most in tune with life. What places did you like to go? What kind of toys did you like to play with? What family activities did you like most? What did you want to be when you grew up? What places did you dream of visiting? What was your biggest dream? What were your hobbies? Continue journaling these thought patterns throughout your school years. Yes, unfortunately, you will recall some pain on this journey. But, I am quite sure you will be surprised at how often you will find yourself smiling and feeling happy, warm emotions you have not felt for years. Journal your experiences of your journey to uncovering your original blueprint and re-discovering you.

Now take the pen or pencil and get out of your own way. Don't think about what you should write but record whatever comes out. You will be surprised about the insight into the inner you, you can discover.

KEYS TO REMEMBER

Let it be fun, relaxing, and insightful. Journaling should be a journey into your inner self. Let it be enlightening. Journal how it helped you reach your goals, come to decisions, and solve problems. Journal about how the process may have helped you to decide to kick that bum out of your life or to finally agree to marry that wonderful partner of 10 years. You will be amazed how journaling will impact your life.

POSITIVE JOURNAL RECAP ACTIVITY

In life, for some reason for many of us, our memory recall tends to remember more of our bad experiences and failures. It is important that you understand the importance and not discount your blessings, good experiences and successes. Many of us use our good experiences to validate and measure the importance and value of our life. For this reason, you need to practice recognizing the good in your life. Start by writing down three positive things or events at the end of each day.

For example:

Monday

1. Kept my workout schedule.
2. Received praise from the manager for work I turned in.
3. The boys didn't bicker at the dinner table.
4. Kept commitment not to buy lunch out.

Repeat this process for each day of the week.

CHAPTER 13
STEP 7: DEFINE YOUR DREAMS AND ASPIRATIONS

OUR CHOICE IS TO continue moving through life aimlessly without a plan and no real purpose or, as Solomon reminds us in this Scripture, planning will lead to abundance. Hasty decision or decisions without adequate planning can lead to poverty.

Start today. Take time to think about what you want and create a plan that will help you reach those goals.

"Goals are the straightest visible path toward your purpose. In order to follow your path, you must first see it. Write your goals down, so you can see your path and follow it to your purpose."
—Sonyia Graham

If you will not invest in yourself, why would you expect someone else to? By taking the time to sit down and write out your goals, you have not only committed to establish some goals for your life, but you have also invested in your future.

"If you fail to plan, you are planning to fail!"
—Benjamin Franklin

"Good planning and hard work lead to prosperity, but hasty shortcuts lead to poverty" (Proverbs 21:5 NLT).

SOFTWARE VS. PEN AND PAPER

Goal and task management can be done using sophisticated software designed explicitly for time and task management. You can also use simple apps like Microsoft Excel and Google Sheets. Twenty years ago, many working professionals used pen and paper via daily and monthly planners available at office supply stores. Others opted for the pricier but wonderfully effective, Franklin Covey system. A casual approach using Post It Notes and a digital list of the matrix we've reviewed is also fine. All of these approaches work. What works best for you depends on the size of your list, lifestyle, willingness to self-govern, self-discipline and a variety of other personal factors. There is no right or best approach beyond following the basic principles we're reviewing. You're likely to find that the more you practice good time management, the more ingrained it becomes and fewer tools/helper apps are needed. It becomes intuitive—natural.

Many of us learned first to ride a bicycle from a tricycle. From there we graduated to two-wheelers with training wheels. Eventually, we mastered the art of balancing ourselves on a moving apparatus without needing extra help. It became natural and instinctive. And if you haven't ridden a bike for years, chances are you can hop back on one and be fine within a few minutes. The same is true with time management and productivity. Once you master it, you don't need as much assistance from external tools. It becomes part of how you think and behave.

SOFTWARE

If you have a large list of responsibilities you want to track, a digital solution is helpful. Ideally, use one that can be accessed from multiple devices if you're leading a hectic and on the go lifestyle. Tastes will vary as to how sophisticated it needs to be for you. Truthfully, if it can capture, prioritize and assign due dates to the things on your To Do List, it's sufficient. Everything else about it is subjective. Reminder alerts and such are nice to have in the beginning.

Here are a few recommendations:

- **30/30** is easy to use and provides everything

you need for task management.

- **135 List** takes a more simplified approach, like the one we've also discussed.
- **Microsoft To-Do** provides task lists that also integrate with Office 365

PEN AND PAPER

The cat is already out of the bag that you can just as easily manage a list with a pen and paper if you're so inclined. This method requires more due diligence on your part. If you're a disciplined and habitual person, it works. If not, you might want software as your tricycle for a little while. In the recommendations that follow, I also include digital writing as pen and paper. However, these aren't special programs for list management. They're simply a blank sheet of digital paper on which you can type.

- **Google Sheet** provides the ability to manage a simple list or matrix. It's free and can be accessed from any device or platform.
- **MS Excel** is like using Google Sheets, but you must own a copy.
- **Sticky Notes** is the digital version of Post It paper. It comes as part of the Windows operating system.
- **Printed Daily Planners** are available in office supply stores.
- **Post It Notes**, or **Index Cards** are placed in order on a cork board, desk or any surface you see on a regular basis. Ideally, where you do most of your work.

GOAL SETTING WORKSHEET

"The first step to getting the things you want out of life is this: Decide what you want."
—Ben Stein

Don't just let life happen, take control of your life by setting goals and taking steps that let you live the life you want. Goals are a type of roadmap that helps you to take steps in the right direction. It is much easier to reach your destination when you have a destination in mind and a roadmap to get you there. Use this worksheet as a starting point to help you set a roadmap for your life. Think about the balance between relationships and accomplishments as well as personal and business. Be careful about sacrificing one area for another over the long term.

INSTRUCTIONS

1. Set aside 30 minutes of time to get started. A place with minimal interruptions will allow you to think and focus. (Some of my best thinking happens when I am alone in the car sitting in parking lots while waiting to pick up my kids.)
2. Read through each of the sections below and use them as a tool to get you started. Add to or adjust the goal categories to make them meaningful to you. The categories we provided are not meant to be a complete list but a starting point you can

expand upon. You are the guide to your own life.
3. Take control and enjoy it!

S.M.A.R.T GOALS

SMART goals are used in situations where measuring the effectiveness of a goal is important for progress. It stands for Specific, Measurable, Attainable, Relevant, and Timely.

Specific: Be specific and clear as you write out your What, Why, and How of your goal. Use strong, powerful action words to state what you are going to do? Know why your goal is important to you and how you are going to do it.

(Example: Instead of saying, "I am going to get into shape," write down that you want to be able to walk three miles at a 20 minute/mile pace, do 20 push-ups and 50 crunches.) Now let's get started.

Measurable: Make sure your goal is measurable. Instead of saying that you want to save more money. Say you want to save $700 for a vacation by putting aside a minimum of $50.00 each month. This way you can see that you are reaching incremental steps as you work towards your goal. Reaching these monthly benchmarks will help keep you motivated as you see progress towards your goal.

Attainable: Make sure that goals you set are realistic and attainable. The goal must be under your control, not someone else's. You want the goal to be something you must work, stretch, and strive to achieve. But not something that is so far out of your reach that you think it's impossible and therefore you never try to reach it.

Relevant: Make sure that the goal you set is a goal you are willing and able to work towards. The goal must be important to you. It should be about you and not someone else. When you think about it, is it worthwhile?

Timely: Make sure that you have a date by when you want to reach your goal otherwise you may say you are working on it, but there will be no urgency to reach it.

The following categories are listed as a guide. Reorganize or add to them as you see fit. Personalize your goal list and make it work for you. You don't have to set goals in all areas at once, so you don't feel overwhelmed. Remember, it is your life; you are in control. You can complete the list and then work on one at a time or several at once. Whatever you do we hope that setting your goals will help you to take control and live the life you want.

SMART GOAL IDEAS

Health & Wellness
Do you want to eat better, lose weight, or get into shape? Do you want to eat healthier by cutting back on some things or increasing your intake of others? You, better than anyone else, know what you want and need in this area.

Lose Weight

- How much?
- By when?
- What's the primary method that will help me achieve it?

Eat Healthier

- How much?
- By when?
- What types of food will I eliminate?

Family and Friends Goals

Are there relationships you would like to strengthen or rekindle? Do you want to reinforce or start family traditions? Are there special events or trips you have put off? Put in writing what you would like to accomplish. Because other people are involved, your goals in this area are dependent on others' participation. With some planning and sharing, your goals may turn into group goals for you and your family and friends. Remember: The most important things in life aren't THINGS!

Improve Family Quality Time

- How much time per week will I dedicate?
- When will I have the schedule in place?
- Things come up, but I'm committed to maintaining this schedule what percent of the time?

Time for Friends

- How frequently can I make time to spend with friends?
- It's important that this time includes which friends?
- I'm committed to making this happen what percentage of the time?

PERSONAL FINANCES

This category includes career, large purchase, home improvement, college/retirement planning, etc. Do you want to save more, spend less, or invest smarter? Setting and reaching financial goals can be very rewarding and also help in reducing your overall stress levels. Here are some ideas or questions to get you started.

Reduce Credit Card Debt

- Reduce my credit card debt by what amount?
- I will achieve this reduction what date?
- By this date, I will have a plan in place that will detail how to accomplish this goal.

Examples of what might be part of the plan:

1. Wait 48 hours before making purchases using a credit card to give me time to evaluate the need and reduce impulse purchases.
2. Instead of purchasing coffee on the way to work, I will make it at home and carry it in a thermos.

3. Reduce the number of discretionary recurring subscriptions I pay for each month such as multiple cable channels, online services, etc.
4. Reduce the number of times per week I eat lunch and dinner out or purchase take-home by half.
5. Establish a monthly personal spending budget that includes clothes, shoes, accessories, entertainment, etc.

SOCIAL, CULTURAL, COMMUNITY & PHILANTHROPY

It's not just about work and family. Other things feed your soul and set the seeds for future blessings.

Expand My Social Circle

- Gain how many new quality acquaintances by when?
- Be able to consider them a part of my circle by when?
- Identify opportunities for meeting new people by when?
- Have attended at least three new functions or gatherings by when?

Start Networking Professionally

- What aspect of my career would benefit most from networking?
- Identify local opportunities to engage in functions by when?

- Have attended at least three new functions or gatherings by when?

Service My Community

- Identify talents, gifts and interests that could serve my community by?
- Match the above with possible community programs by?
- Contact the program leaders by?
- I will offer my time as a volunteer to my preferred organization by?

PERSONAL GOALS

Remember that considering your personal needs and ambitions doesn't make you selfish, it makes you a well-rounded and adjusted human being. Therefore, your goals should also include things that benefit you as a person. Explore what matters to you. Be sure to consider travel, mental stimulation, education, spiritual, or whatever else, is important to you.

LONG-TERM GOALS

Many goals we set are those we hope to accomplish in less than one year. Be sure to also set some long-term goals for two, five and even ten years down the line. Picture how you want your life to be and set goals to guide you. Write out steps and timelines of how you will reach these goals. You don't complete a bucket list by only focusing on the listed end-game objectives. There are many small milestone goals along the way. Setting these long-term goals will help you to live your life on your terms, instead of just letting life happen.

CHAPTER 14
STEP 8: BUCKET LIST 101

EVERYONE SHOULD HAVE A Bucket List. It's not only for naming movies or for the rich. To live a rewarding, inspired and fulfilling life, you must feed your desires and ambitions. Merely hoping or praying for something to happen, won't bring it about. The Lord helps those who help themselves. If you don't have a Bucket List, now's a perfect time to begin establishing one.

5 EASY STEPS TO STARTING YOUR "BUCKET LIST"

1. Set aside at least 30 minutes to start the process of making your Bucket List. Start out by setting a goal of coming up with at least 10 items. It may be harder than you think. Remember this list is something you will add to over your lifetime.

2. To start your list, write categories such as travel, career, family, financial, health, and random

at the top of separate pages. These sections are a start and can be changed as needed. Ask yourself questions about each section. What would you like to accomplish in your career? What would you like to see and do before you "kick the bucket?" Ask yourself what you would like to do if you only had one year to live? Make sure you add items that YOU want to accomplish and would enjoy not what others think would be exciting. Your friends may want to scuba dive the Great Barrier Reef but if you are not one who enjoys the ocean then don't add it to your list. Really think about stuff you have dreamed of doing. The things that make you happy just thinking about them. Think about where you want to be in two, five, and ten years. Be sure to list smaller less dramatic items as well. Every dream does not have to be to travel across the world or to risk your life. Items on your bucket list can be as simple as to get together with an old friend and to laugh until you cry. These smaller more easily attainable goals make the list more fun and encouraging while you are saving up for that world cruise.

3. Review the list items often to either add to them or to make sure that you still want to do them. Remember that a bucket list is open-ended and ever-changing. As your life changes so will your goals and dreams. Make sure you stay flexible so that you don't become a slave to your list. Keep working on adding new items while completing others.

4. Find ways to make your goals more meaningful. Running a 1/2 marathon is a great accomplishment but doing it with a group as a fundraiser for a good cause may make it even more memorable. Visiting the Eiffel Tower with your child because they recently graduated with a degree in French may mean more than purchasing a package through your travel agent and heading there next summer.

5. Now plan and enjoy the process. Most experts in the field acknowledge that planning is a requirement of setting and achieving goals. Look at your bucket list and pick one of the items on that list. Write a short list of steps you would have to take to make that dream a reality. Get started on making that dream a reality by doing one of the steps within the next 24 hours. The step could be to make a budget, so you know how you will save up for that trip to Europe or go out and purchase a book on great places to visit while in Paris. Your first step could be as simple as picking a weekend next month to finally go to that Fine Arts Museum that you have talked about for the last five years. The important thing is to do something that will get you one step closer to fulfilling that dream.

Just remember that setting your focus on what's most important to you will bring your life purpose and a sense of accomplishment. It will help you to rediscover the real you!

STARTER BUCKET LIST

If you only had one year to live, what would you do in that time? List the top five things and continue to add to this list as you accomplish things on your bucket list.

1. _____

2. _____

3. _____

TRAVEL - Where would you like to go?

1. _____

2. _____

3. _____

4. _____

5. _____

CAREER - What do you want to accomplish?

1. _____

2. _____

3. _____

   _____

4. _____

   _____

FAMILY - What would you like to see family-wise?

1. _____

   _____

2. _____

   _____

3. _____

   _____

4. _____

   _____

5. _____

   _____

FINANCIAL- Where would you like to be financially?

1. _____

   _____

2. _____

   _____

3. _____

   _____

4. _____

   _____

5. _____

   _____

HEALTH - What would you like to change health-wise?

1. _____

2. _____

3. _____

4. _____

5. _____

CHAPTER 15

STEP 9: YOUR GIFTS AND TALENTS

MOST PEOPLE CAN LEARN almost anything with hard work and perseverance. Once you learn a new skill you can become pretty good at it. But, something you were created to do and have an extraordinary talent for is a gift. A gift is something you do not have to learn or work at that is a natural part of you. The best part of gifts and talents are they are usually things you are passionate about, enjoy doing, and you are GREAT at them! Of course, you can improve in areas of your gifts and it does not feel like work because you enjoy it.

"A man's gifts make room for him and bring him before great men"
(Proverbs 18:16 – 16).

Choose a job you love, and you will never have to
work a day in your life.
—**Confucius.**

By uncovering your gifts and talents, you can operate in them and enjoy the benefits. Are you still searching for that dream job? Are you still trying to decide what you want to be when you grow up? You are not alone. Many of us go from job to job trying to find that right career for us. Part of the problem is that we have not identified our talents as gifts. Once you have identified your gifts you can properly assign them to your future.

Do what you love, and the money will follow
—**Marsha Sinetar**

BEGIN UNCOVERING YOURS

Answer and explain the questions below to discover your talents and gifts:

1. What subjects do you get excited about and could go on talking about them for hours?

    _____
    _____
    _____
    _____

2. You are happiest when?

_____

_____

_____

_____

3. What do you get a lot of compliments about?

_____

_____

_____

_____

4. What activity or activities have you noticed you were good at since childhool?

_____

_____

_____

_____

5. What activity or activities have you received acknowledgements and awards for?

_____

_____

_____

_____

6. What special skills do you have?

_____

_____

_____

_____

7. Do people confide in you often?

_____

_____

_____

_____

8. Are you very organized?

_____

_____

_____

_____

9. Are you a hands-on person?

_____

_____

_____

_____

10. Are you creative?

_____

_____

_____

_____

11. Are you a good cook?

_____

_____

_____

_____

12. Do you get enjoyment by using your hands to fix and build things?

_____
_____
_____
_____

13. Are you good at doing research?

_____
_____
_____
_____
_____

14. Are you computer savvy?

_____
_____
_____
_____

15. Do you enjoy speaking in front of groups?

_____
_____
_____
_____

16. Are you great with fashion, style and/ or coordinating wardrobes?

_____
_____
_____
_____

17. Are you a good listener?

_____
_____
_____
_____

18. Do people seek you for advice?

_____
_____
_____
_____

19. Do you get people laughing without trying?

_____
_____
_____
_____

20. Do you recycle and are you passionate about making changes in the environment?

_____
_____
_____
_____

21. Do you love to volunteer?

_____
_____
_____
_____

22. Are you photogenic?

_____

_____

_____

_____

23. Do you have a great eye for photography?

_____

_____

_____

_____

24. Have you ever invented anything?

_____

_____

_____

_____

25. Are you a great writer?

_____

_____

_____

_____

26. Do you love to tell stories?

_____

_____

_____

_____

27. Are you a big facts person?

_____

_____

_____

_____

28. Do you like taking on other characters or acting?

_____

_____

_____

_____

29. Do you love to watch DIY shows?

_____

_____

_____

_____

30. Do you have an innovative or creative mind?

_____

_____

_____

_____

31. What are you passionate about?

_____

_____

_____

_____

32. Did you re-discover anything about yourself while doing this exercise that you may have forgotten?

_____

_____

_____

_____

CHAPTER 16
STEP 10: LIFE IS TOO SHORT!

LIFE IS TOO SHORT … every day get up to enjoy it while you are still breathing. Enjoy every single moment that life offers you. Avoid being pessimistic which will only make you remember the negative sides and block you from focusing on solutions for major problems that impede you from cultivating the state of your happiness.

"I love them that love me; and those that seek me early shall find me"
(Proverbs 8:17 – 17).

ALWAYS BE OPTIMISTIC

Optimism towards life is an important step to achieve happiness. Life is dynamic. We go through good and bad times, ups and downs and still have the strength to overcome its variation. Live life with great expectancy of an amazing life and future.

"But those who hope in the Lord will renew their strength. They will soar on wings like eagles; they will run and not grow weary, they will walk and not be faint"
(Isaiah 40:31).

LET GO OF THE PAST

Always stay focused on your present and look ahead to your future. If you have gone through a lot of disappointment, uneasiness, suffering, and pain in the past, this does not mean your present will be filled by the same painful moments. Forget about the past that will interfere with you making any progress in your life. You should look towards the present and your surroundings and plan a fulfilled life of joy while fulfilling God's purpose for your life.

"For I know the plans I have for you. "declares the Lord. "plans to prosper you and not to harm you, plans to give you hope and a future"
(Jeremiah 29:11).

NEW BEGINNINGS DAILY

Some days you may regress. It's okay. Start again. By beginning each day with a clean slate with no regrets, blame, or feelings of defeat, you will evolve and you will walk in the fact that you are a precious multi-faceted gift from God.

"The steadfast love of the Lord never ceases; his mercies never come to an end; they are new every morning; great is your faithfulness" (Lamentations 3:22-23).

HOW WILL YOU BE REMEMBERED?

As you're living your life and impacting those around you, ask yourself how do you want to be remembered? Contemplating your legacy, the accomplishments that live on after you pass is key in resolving your reason for being. "Imagine your grandchildren talking to their grandchildren about you. What would they say? Would they say you were generous and kind? Would they say you were reliable?"

Ask yourself these questions to help guide you toward your purpose. The questions will lay the groundwork you will need ensure you will be proudly remembered for these things. Remember to take into consideration how these things are received and viewed by others. It is not only what you think. To help this exercise along, remember your mentors and role models, the people you admire and respect. And consider if you are currently exhibiting any of these behaviors or characteristics.

What could you create or do, that will impact people and the world for years to come?

Maybe you can write a book. The written word is a time capsule of sorts because many different generations can pick up that same book. It may read different to them but at the same time depending on the genre it could still remain relevant and useful.

"Do not merely listen to the word, and so deceive yourself. Do what the word says"
(James 1:22).

PART 3: LIVE YOUR BEST LIFE

In this section, you will find more in-depth information and resources for areas of your life that are important to the process of moving in a positive, healthy direction so that you can experience life with fulfillment and joy the way you were meant to experience it while fulfilling God's purpose for your life.

CHAPTER 17
TAKE CARE OF YOURSELF

"AS AN OLYMPIAN, I have learned the importance of taking care of my body. A lot of people think it is only the training that gets you to the next level. It is, in fact, the things we do outside the gym that make the biggest difference. It is all about what you eat and drink, how you work, and how you sleep. At the Olympic Training Center, some of the things mentioned in this book are the main items given to the high-level athletes. Now that I am retired, I have found this is the same formula I use to maintain a healthy and productive lifestyle. My diet is a priority. I teach the value of good food to my daughter. I also stay active, not just in the gym, but as a lifestyle. Lastly, I value my sleep and don't allow anything to prevent it. I understand my body is here for a greater purpose and I must treat it the best I can so God can get the best out of it."
—Nia Nicole Abdallah, 2004 Olympic Silver Medalist, And National Team Coach

Taking care of yourself, emotionally and physically, plays a role in how you live. To accomplish your best, you must be at your best. The following questions will indicate how well you are taking care of yourself.

1. How is your health? Does it reflect or affect your purpose?

   _____

   _____

   _____

2. Do you eat breakfast, lunch, and dinner?

   _____

   _____

   _____

3. Do you exercise or workout a minimum of 30 minutes at least three times a week?

   _____

   _____

   _____

4. Do you drink water?

   _____

   _____

   _____

5. Do you get 8 hours of sleep a night?

   _____

   _____

   _____

Your health is one of the key factors in your purpose. What does God mean when He says our bodies are our temples?

"Do you not know that your bodies are temples of the Holy Spirit, who is in you, whom you have received from God? You are not your own; you were bought at a price. Therefore, honor God with your bodies"
(1 Corinthians 6:19-20).

"Don't you know that you yourselves are God's temple and that God's Spirit dwells in your midst? 17 if anyone destroys God's temple, God will destroy that person; for God's temple is sacred and you together are the temple"
(1 Corinthians 3:16-17).

"Therefore, I urge you, brothers and sisters, in view of God's mercy, to offer your bodies as a living sacrifice, holy and pleasing to God - this is your true and proper worship"
(Romans 12:1-2).

"So whether you eat or drink or whatever you do, do it all for the glory of God"
(1 Corinthians 10:31).

During my 11-year journey, I was a certified personal trainer and director for a personal training company. This role blessed me with the ability and opportunity to help change lives. It taught me that health and fitness are key to one's preservation, longevity, and quality of life and that the alternative to this is death. Without your life, everything else is void. Game over.

Although we're discussing general guidelines suitable for all adults; you should always consult your physician before making lifestyle changes related to health and nutrition, especially if you're on medication or have received a diagnosis of a chronic condition.

THE BASICS OF GOOD NUTRITION

There are five components of healthy nutrition:

1. Eat at least 5-6 small meals per day (eating every 2-3 hours.)
2. Do not eat refined foods, especially sugar (healthy foods are minimally processed whole foods that are close to the natural state.)
3. Watch your fat intake (watch amount and type of fat you are ingesting, Trans fat is the worst fat.)
4. Drink plenty of water (every cell, and single life supporting biochemical reaction that goes on inside the body requires water. (Drink half your body weight in ounces/day.)
5. Proper supplementation American Medical Association's position is that "doctors should recommend that all patients, even healthy ones, routinely take vitamins and mineral supplements. All vitamins and minerals should come from whole foods with at least 100% of the recommended daily allowances, NEVER synthetic replications.

(Six Essential Nutrients)

1. Proteins - each gram of protein has approximately 4 calories - used mostly in your body for tissue and organ repair - 12% to 25% of total calories/day
2. Carbohydrates - each gram of carbohydrates has approximately four calories - used mostly by your body for energy - 50% to 60% of total calories/day
3. Fats - each gram of fats has approximately nine calories - used to protect organs, for energy, and to aid in the absorption of vitamins - 10 to 30% of total calories/day
4. Vitamins - 0 calories - necessary for proper growth and maintenance and health
5. Minerals - 0 calories - vital for the physical and mental well-being
6. Water - 0 calories - water consumption is vital for the conversion of fat to energy - helps to clean the body of toxins - should drink half your body weight in ounces of water/day

Get some help and support to hold you accountable.

BENEFITS OF A PERSONAL TRAINER

Having a professional in your corner can be a huge motivating factor for some people. If you need encouragement, advice or a voice cheering you forward, a personal trainer can help.

Many people dismiss the idea of hiring a personal trainer because of pride (they think they should already know how to stay in condition), shame over their physical condition, or because of the cost. It is an investment in your health and your quality of life. What good is money if you are not healthy and fit?

Consider the following 10 Reasons for hiring a personal trainer:

1. Motivation—Perhaps the single, most significant benefit of hiring a trainer is motivation. On their own, people lose motivation to stick with a consistent exercise program. A certified fitness trainer can provide structure, direction, accountability and a friend who is interested in helping you succeed.

2. Individualized Program—Too many people shy away from the gym, or from any exercise because of chronic health conditions or injuries. A trainer will work with you and your healthcare provider to construct a safe and effective program to reach your health goals.

3. Efficiency —The job of a personal trainer is to keep you focused on results. No wasted, ineffectual workouts. A personal trainer will devise a plan to help you get maximum results in minimum time.

4. Improve Technical Skill—Every profession has its specialists, and a trainer who specializes in sports-specific training will help you improve your skills by showing you a new training technique specific to your sport. Whether it is golf, hockey, baseball, long distance running, or

whatever ... your trainer will incorporate skills training into your program to improve not only your strength and endurance but your agility and mental focus as well.

5. New to Exercise—If you're an absolute beginner, a personal trainer is the ultimate fitness coach. Save yourself a lot of wasted time and futile effort and frustration by having a program designed by a trainer. Not only will you gain strength and lose fat more quickly, but you will do it safely and with an understanding of what you are doing each step of the way. You will be able to go into any gym with confidence that you know what you are doing.

6. Breakthrough Plateaus—Perhaps you are in good shape already, but you haven't been able to progress beyond a certain point. If you are stuck in the same routine and want to break out of a rut, a trainer is a perfect solution. A trainer will jump start, not only your motivation but your routine as well.

7. Short-Term Mentoring—If you ultimately want to learn to be able to work out on your own so you don't need to use a trainer, going for a few months may be all you need. All good trainers will teach you the basics of building and modify a fitness program for you to achieve maximum results.

8. Workout Safely—A trainer watches your form, monitors your vitals, and can provide objective feedback about your limits and strengths. Most of us tend to ignore some of the subtle signals our body produces. We either push through pain or

141

give up too soon. Because a trainer watches what you are doing while you are doing it, they can help push you or slow you down as necessary.

9. Workout at Home—Many trainers make house calls. If you don't have the time or interest in going to a gym but have a hard time knowing what to do on your own at home, a personal trainer can bring fitness into your living room.

10. Weight Loss Support—The number one reason people hire personal trainers is to lose weight and get into shape because, well ... it works. If you made a resolution to lose the fat and build muscle, a trainer can keep you on track and help you realize that goal.

BENEFITS OF STRENGTH TRAINING

Burn 500 calories a day while resting! Did you know that by adding one pound of muscle mass to your body you will burn 50 calories a day at rest? By adding 10 pounds of muscle mass to your body you will burn 500 calories a day at rest. Let's do the math. If you burn 500 calories a day at rest seven days a week, you will burn 3500 calories a week at rest, and that is roughly one pound of fat a week. Not too bad for non-activity weight management. That's why it's important to change your body mass by adding muscle. Remember to always consult your physician before starting any physical fitness program.

I do understand there are myths and misconceptions about weight training. Let's look at a couple of them.

MYTHS OF STRENGTH TRAINING

Ladies, you don't need to worry about looking like a man. Strength training doesn't necessitate getting bulky. Remember, your bodyweight depends on the number of calories you eat and use. Strength training will make you gain muscle and lose fat. But you'll stay at the same bodyweight unless you start eating more.

Women also have lower testosterone levels than men. Muscle mass and strength depend on your testosterone levels. The only way women can get as muscular as men is by using steroids or prohormones. If you'd like to learn more about strength training you can visit Stronglifts.com.

The other reason to consider strength training is as you get older you lose muscle mass and you will need strength and flexibility. Yes, even to get out of the bed and help combat against falls and other things that can come with age. So, ladies don't be afraid to pick up that dumbbell.

FIVE PARTS OF PHYSICAL FITNESS

Physical fitness is the ability to function effectively throughout your day, perform all your usual activities, and still have enough energy left over to handle any extra stresses or emergencies which may arise.

The components of physical fitness are:

1. Cardiorespiratory (CR) endurance — the efficiency with which the body delivers oxygen and nutrients needed for muscular activity and

transports waste products from the cells.

2. Muscular strength—the greatest amount of force a muscle or muscle group can exert in a single effort.

3. Muscular endurance—the ability of a muscle or muscle group to perform repeated movements with a sub-maximal force for extended periods of times.

4. Flexibility—the ability to move the joints or any group of joints through an entire, normal range of motion.

5. Body composition—the percentage of body fat a person has in comparison to his or her total body mass.

Improving the first three components of fitness listed above will have a positive impact on body composition and will result in less fat. Excessive body fat detracts from the other fitness components, reduces performance, detracts from appearance, and negatively affects your health.

Factors such as speed, agility, muscle power, eye-hand coordination, and eye-foot coordination are classified as components of "motor" fitness. These factors most affect your athletic ability. Appropriate training can improve these factors within the limits of your potential. A sensible weight loss and fitness program seeks to improve or maintain all the components of physical and motor fitness through sound, progressive, mission specific physical training.

PRINCIPLES OF EXERCISE

Adherence to specific basic exercise principles is essential for developing an effective program. The same principles of exercise apply to everyone at all levels of physical training, from the Olympic-caliber athlete to the weekend jogger.

These basic principles of exercise must be followed.

- Regularity—To achieve a training effect, you must exercise often. You should exercise each of the first four fitness components at least three times a week. Infrequent exercise can do more harm than good. Regularity is also important in resting, sleeping, and following a sensible diet.
- Progression—The intensity (how hard) and/or duration (how long) of exercise must gradually increase to improve the level of fitness.
- Balance—To be effective, a program should include activities that address all the fitness components, since overemphasizing any one of them may hurt the others.
- Variety—Providing a variety of activities reduces boredom and increases motivation and progress.
- Specificity—Training must be geared toward specific goals. For example, people become better runners if their training emphasizes running. Although swimming is great exercise, it does not improve a two-mile-run time as much as a running program does.
- Recovery—A hard day of training for a given component of fitness should be followed by an

easier training day or rest day for that component and/or muscle groups to help permit recovery. Another way to allow recovery is to alternate the muscle groups exercised every other day, especially when training for strength and/or muscle endurance.

- Overload—The workload of each exercise session must exceed the normal demands placed on the body to bring about a training effect.

You have learned about taking care of yourself, now just do it.

CHAPTER 18
TIME MANAGEMENT

HOW WELL DO YOU manage your time? Let's explore if the way you currently handle your time reflects or affects your purpose.

"The purpose of time management and getting more done in less time is to enable you to spend more face time with the people you care about and doing the things that give you the greatest amount of joy in life."
—Brian Tracy

Questions:

1. Do you have work-life balance? _____

2. Do you have time to hang out with family and friends? _____

3. Do you accomplish what you desire to each day?_____

4. Do you sometimes feel there is not enough time in your day to accomplish things? _____

If you answered yes to any of these, you might want to take a closer look at this. Perhaps the greatest single problem people have today is "time poverty." Working people have too much to do and too little time for their personal lives. Most people feel overwhelmed with responsibilities and activities, and the harder they work, the further behind they feel. Instead of clearly deciding what they want to do, they continually react to what is happening around them. Pretty soon they lose all sense of control.

Time is your most precious resource. It is the most valuable thing you have. Time is perishable and irreplaceable. It cannot be saved. It can only be reallocated from activities of lower value to activities of higher value. All work requires time. The act of taking a moment to think about your time before you spend it will immediately improve your personal time management and increase productivity. I used to think that time management was only a business tool, like Outlook, something you use at work to be more productive which could eventually lead to more pay. Then I learned that time management is not a peripheral activity or skill. It is the core skill upon which everything else in life depends.

IMPORTANCE OF PERSONAL GOALS

You can improve your overall productivity by setting personal goals. In your work or business life, there are so many demands on your time from other people that little of your time is yours to use as you choose. However, at home, you can exert a tremendous amount of control over how you use your time and increase productivity throughout the day in your personal life. Time-management begins with you. It starts with your thinking through what is important to you. You need to set goals in three major areas of your life.

First, you need family and personal goals. These are the reasons why you get up in the morning, why you work hard and upgrade your skills, why you worry about money and sometimes feel frustrated by the demands on your time. What are your family and personal goals, both tangible and intangible? A tangible family goal could be a bigger house, a better car, a larger television set, a vacation, or anything else that costs money. An intangible goal would be to build a higher quality relationship with your mate and children, to spend more time with your family by going for walks or reading books. Achieving these family and personal goals are the real essences of time management and its major purpose. For more information on personal goals, visit www.briantracy.com.

ARE YOU TOO AVAILABLE?

In our day-to-day lives, we operate on schedules with everything from doctor appointments, work, and school. There must be a good reason for them. If you are scheduling a business meeting, you give options for availability, such as I am available between 2 and 4 p.m. on Monday. Unfortunately, we do not carry this over to our day-to-day life and relationships. Here is what tends to happen.

In this exercise, fill in the blank spaces below with your name.

Someone mentions that they need you to volunteer and you reply: "Sure, just let me know when." Now you have left yourself wide open, and in many cases over obligated. You now find yourself saying, "Why did I say yes?" You are now experiencing anxiety on when it will happen, complaining and stressing because you gave up your time and power blindly.

Let's try this scenario again:

"_____, could you come help us out and volunteer?" Your new answer: "Sure I am available on Tuesdays and Wednesdays between noon and 3 pm." Now you did not give away any power, and you had a voice and an active role in making the commitment and will know what you are doing and when. By not scheduling life, you can also miss out on things that mean a lot to you. How many times have you and close friends or relatives said let's get together soon, but it never happens. You want it to happen and have the best intentions of making it happen when you say it. But, neither party seems to find the time. Your childhood friend says, let's get together soon." You reply, "That would be great, I miss hanging out."

Let's try this scenario again:

"_____, it has been a year since we have seen each other, when can we get together?" Your new answer is "I am available every other Saturday between 2 and 4. When could we hang out?"

I am not saying you will always make these dates work. However, if you establish a date, you'll have something to work towards even if it's rescheduled a few times before it happens.

Appearing too available to prospective suitors will not establish the right value or self-worth.

When a suitor says, "I want to take you out" or "I want to get together with you," and you say, "Sure let me know," you are basically saying, "I do not have a life, and I will be awaiting your call for plans." You never want to appear that accessible. Remember, you do have your own life, and if you don't, I need you to re-read the chapter on Living a Full Life.

Push rewind and let's try it again:

A suitor says, "I want to take you out." Your new answer: "Sounds great. I am available next Saturday evening, what do you have in mind?" Now they are thinking, *Wow! They have a life, and I cannot assume they are waiting around for me.* That's powerful. But, let's not get it twisted. I am not saying play games with any suitor's emotions. I am trying to show you, the power you have and how to use it. As a result, they now know you have a life, even if your plans only involve watching Netflix by yourself.

Bonus: You just used your power to move that event from who knows when to next week. That's powerful! The best way to set the tone and get someone to respect your time is to show them that it's not unlimited. Your schedule should not always be the one that is fair weather and subject to change. There's no reason that when schedule concession needs to be made it is always your schedule that must be considered flexible and movable. Many people tend to position themselves this way to fix things and make things work. I think I've heard it called the Superwoman/Superman syndrome.

CHAPTER 19
ME TIME

WE ALL NEED ALONE time, and you don't have to break the bank to get it. You can have meaningful relaxation and rejuvenation time right in your own home.

Life events make you rethink your priorities. They make you think about slowing down and enjoying life rather than always focusing on the rat race we call life.

Most of us are over-worked, over-scheduled and stressed out. We know we need to slow down, but it is not always easy to find the time or money to get away. A tropical island or secluded lodge sound nice but may be currently out of reach. Here are some ideas to help you enjoy a getaway closer to home. You can even include your family or friends in your retreat or arrange your schedule so that you have two hours of uninterrupted bliss in your new getaway.

CREATE AN OUTDOOR RETREAT

Sometimes we need to get away from our everyday responsibilities but don't have the time or opportunity to get in the car and drive away from it all. Give yourself the chance to enjoy a getaway by creating your own outdoor paradise. Use your garden, patio, or balcony to create a nature retreat. Arrange different types of plants to create a beautiful and serene setting. Think about including plants that will attract butterflies to add to nature's beauty. Use your retreat when you need a dose of nature to relax and refocus your life. Be sure to get yourself a comfortable lawn chair or chaise lounge to take full advantage of your new outdoor paradise. Use the time to care for your plants as short ME time moments to also tune out your daily demands.

PAMPER YOURSELF

Do you like bubble baths, having massages, sitting in a sauna or jacuzzi, manicures or facials? If this is you, create your own spa retreat box. Purchase great smelling bubble baths, reinvigorating scrubs, body treatments, a bath brush, and Loofah. Make sure you pick up some facial treatments, foot soaks, soothing lotions, all the manicure tools like a professional. Pick up an inflatable bath pillow and comfortable bathrobe if you like. Organize all your items in a special "spa retreat container" you can tuck away in your closet. Once every month or two schedule time to pamper yourself. The expense of all your items will last you the entire year and will be less than getting one treatment at a spa.

HAVE A MOVIE NIGHT

Turn a movie night into a retreat. Have blankets, pillows, popcorn, snacks and your favorite drink. Pick a movie you want to see not something someone else picked or brought home. Two hours of downtime is all you need. Of course, you can invite some friends as some movies are meant to be shared.

MINI ARTIST STUDIO

Do you have an artistic side but never get to express it? Go out and purchase the supplies you need. Get a sketch pad, drawing pencils, watercolors, paint brushes, canvases, an easel, or whatever supplies you need. Store supplies in an easily accessible container. Schedule a date with yourself to set up and focus on your artwork for an hour or two. Draw something from nature, a still life, or ask a friend to join you and draw her portrait. Focusing on a piece of art can be calming and help reduce stress. If you have the room, you can designate a spot in front of a window as your studio where your supplies will be easily accessible anytime you have a moment to yourself.

CHEF'S KITCHEN

If cooking or baking is your passion, then turn your kitchen into your retreat. Treat yourself to that mixer you have always wanted. Buy the unique ingredients for that dish or the cookbook that has the recipe you want to try. Find the time to cook or bake without interruption.

Cook or bake that special dish for the fun of cooking not because you must. Take the time to savor your dish by yourself or loved ones. Make the time enjoyable and relaxing for you.

DO IT YOURSELF (DIY)

Maybe you enjoy watching the DIY Channel and have always wanted to attempt a project. Go out and buy the supplies for the project and get started. Once you have completed the project, you'll bask in a sense of accomplishment.

You can also investigate taking a day trip or weekend getaway close to home. Spending a day outdoors fishing, hiking at a local park, enjoying a festival or public concert to get away from your day to day obligations. Paying for one night in a hotel can turn a typical weekend into a romantic getaway that can add a spark to a relationship. Plan to spend your entire weekend away. You can include visits to museums or a romantic walk in the park. Look for places that are within two to four hours driving distance to get you out of your everyday environment while keeping costs to a minimum. Start looking for destinations and activities within your area. I am sure you will be amazed at what is in close proximity to you. No matter what you do or how you spend your time, slow down and enjoy your life.

Waste your money and you're only out of money
but waste your time and you've lost a part of your
life.
—Michael Leboeuf

In the lines below, write down five activities you
can do to escape the stress of everyday life.

1. _____
   _____
2. _____
   _____
3. _____
   _____
4. _____
   _____
5. _____
   _____

BEST MOTHER'S DAY EVER
BY ILONA RANSOM

Me Time and bucket list items look different for each of us. Near drowning, a sore butt and wobbly legs are what looked good to me for Mother's Day. We have decided to make this our ME year. Besides launching our platform and book, we have decided to work on our own personal "Bucket List" items and on making sure we find our own ME time on a regular basis.

Recently I had the chance to do something I wanted to do. I got to mark one item off my bucket list. Since it was Mother's Day, I got my girls to participate with me in a Mini Sprint Triathlon. Yes, a triathlon and yes, I bribed them. Please keep your eye on the Mini Sprint part of this event.

We got up at 4:30 a.m. to get ready and make it across town to check in by 6:30 a.m. Once we arrived, we were lost and confused on how everything worked so we walked back and forth to the check-in area several times. By 6:45 we had our race numbers clearly marked on our legs and arms, our bikes parked in the appropriate spot, and we were standing by the edge of the boat ramp at the lake waiting for the race to start.

My heart was pounding as the horn sounded and my age group raced into the water. Arms and legs were going everywhere. I felt myself kicking people behind me at the same time I was trying to avoid the arms and legs in front and on the sides of me. Three quarters through the 200-yard open lake swim (yes, only 200 yards) I thought my arms were going to fall off. When I could see people were starting to walk about 20 feet ahead of me I talked myself through the slow-moving last strokes. The ground beneath my feet could not get there quick enough.

I climbed out of the water and removed my fashionable purple swim cap and goggles as I jogged to the bike staging area. In less than 3.5 minutes I dried off, put on shoes, socks, shorts, and shirt, fastened my helmet and headed out for a nice 8-mile bike ride. My 10-year-old mountain bike was clinking and clanking as I peddled along. Even though I wasn't racing at top speeds, at the time I thought I was pushing myself. The multitude of bikers that slipped by me on their smooth humming street racing bikes yelled out encouragement that made me smile and kept me going. I jumped off my bike as I completed that portion of the race only to realize my legs were quite rubbery. I used my bike as support to hold myself up as I proceeded to the transition area.

I quickly took off my helmet, grabbed my water bottle and started out on the final leg of the race, the 2-mile run. Well, I am not much of a runner so for me this was a 2-mile walk. I crossed the finish line at 1 hour 8 minutes and 55 seconds (1:08.55). A great finish I thought for someone who signed up seven days before the race. I felt a great sense of accomplishment and pride for attempting and completing the race. I enjoyed the fact I did this with my daughters as it is a memory we will share and talk about for years. I am happy that I did something for myself, something that pushed my limits and comfort zone. Something that made me feel good about myself. As I sit here sipping tea out of my finisher's cup, I know that I will cherish this Mother's Day memory forever.

ME TIME IDEAS

Fill this section out with some Me time ideas.

_____

_____

_____

_____

_____

_____

_____

_____

_____

Have you ever gone to the grocery store and roamed the aisles aimlessly without a care in the world? Your mind is almost blank; it feels like an out of body experience. You seem to be moving in slow motion. Before you know it, you have spent hours in the store, and it seems like a blur. You can't even recall what the heck you have been doing because you are still missing the milk and bread you wanted to get in the first place. Well, you just took a grocery store get away.

Sometimes your mind decides it needs the getaway time you neglected to plan. You weren't even aware you were taking it, while leisurely meandering up and down the aisles. Wow! That is pretty pathetic. Surely, we can find a better way to spend our much-needed ME time. Don't wait until your mind forces you to take the ME Time it needs. When was the last time you had a grocery store getaway or other unusual ways you may have grabbed a few minutes of ME Time?

CHAPTER 20
EXPAND YOUR HORIZON

"LIVING AND LOVING LIFE enable you to expand your horizons in so many ways. At the age of 70, I am the oldest female BMX racer in the United States. When at the age of 40, there were those who wanted to know why I wanted to race bicycle motocross, as this was a sport typical of boys, men, and girls. My son and husband delved into the sport, with my cheering them on as I stood on the sidelines.

As a recreational cyclist, I realized that BMX racing would provide an opportunity for me to challenge myself at a greater level and develop that core strength and core stability that would enable me to become a competitive racer. Because of continued persistence and perseverance throughout the past 30 years, BMX racing has become my life-fulfilling passion. I have developed the skills and techniques that have resulted in my earning local, state, national and international accolades as a BMX racer.

By working with the BMX sanctioning bodies, the rules were changed to include women classes. Now

thousands of women throughout the United States, as well as other nations, have joined the ranks of BMX racing. In expanding my horizons, I have empowered not only myself but women throughout the world to compete in a sport that brings me, and them, great joy."
—Kittie Weston-Knauer, Bmx Racing Champion, And Educator

We all need to get out and try something new. Have you always thought yoga looked interesting or martial arts would be fun? Do you enjoy gardening but are never sure of when those roses should be trimmed or fertilized? Would you like to create a family website but don't know where to begin?

To pick up a hobby, learn something new, or refine your skills look no further than your local neighborhood newspaper or flyer. I recently looked at our local flyer and found meeting times for a gardening club, art classes, a hurricane readiness class, an Emergency Preparedness Seminar as well as a list of new classes and activities offered by our local YMCA. I then went online and looked up our local library and found that they regularly offered adult activities including computer classes, book clubs, movie nights, Spanish classes and game nights. Most if not all activities at our library were offered free of charge.

In our city, Houston, we also can take all types of classes through Adult Learning Classes. You can take courses in just about any subject that interest you like cooking classes such as Under the Tuscan Sun and Vegan Organics 101. You can improve your writing by taking "Ain't" Writing Fun? A Grammar and Writing Refresher or the Basics of Screenwriting. You can take courses such as Blues Piano, Beginning Guitar I & II, Public Speaking for the Chicken-Hearted or Basics of Bridge. Of course, there is a long list of computer courses as well as classes in auto mechanics, basic boating, martial arts, and legal as well as financial matters. I think you get the point that you can find courses in all kinds of subject matters ... . These courses do have a charge, but they are a great way to learn more about one of those interests you have neglected to pursue.

So, quit sitting at home and making excuses. Expand your horizon by looking into one activity this month.

EMPOWER YOURSELF

You may have to put your career on hold or delay it, to take care of the family. It is a beautiful thing to do and many times for the right reasons. Unfortunately, due to the value that domestication tends to carry many lose their position of contribution to the household and are made to feel that they are now in debt to the person that is now earning the household income, for being allowed to stay home and take care of the family. Maybe even hearing this statement from time to time, "Because of me!" from the income earner. Would it be fair to say that because of you taking care of children and household the income earner is free to go out and work to provide for the household?

Speaking first hand some people are, stay at home parents but have a business or a side hustle. Some work their regular jobs at home. Maybe some are not contributing financially as much as they use to but contributing something while keeping the household together and providing hands-on stability for the children. So now tell me, how many jobs a person has that stays home to take care of the household?

1. Caring for the children
2. Chauffeuring children to activities
3. Attending children events
4. Volunteering to nurture partnerships with teachers at your child's school
5. Taking care of the house
6. Getting food for the household
7. Preparing meals for the family

I am not taking credit away from the one who goes to work outside the household. I commend the person who is taking care of their household financially because that is decent and in order. It is also biblical.

"Anyone who does not provide for their relatives, and especially for their own household, has denied the faith and is worse than an unbeliever" (1 Timothy 5:8 NIV).

In this previous verse, Paul is speaking to the entire church. Those who can provide for their families are obligated to do so biblically. Now it is time to empower yourself. The importance of re-establishing your self-worth and creating some security is crucial in rediscovering yourself. There are many things you can do to fulfill this quest. Here are a few listed below and some resources.

START YOUR OWN BUSINESS

Have you ever wanted to work from home or start your own business? Is it your dream to work for yourself or create a second stream of income?

Many resources can help you get started or assist you along the way. You may find this list of resources helpful. I am not endorsing their services.

Please research companies carefully before contracting with them to do business. Also due to the nature of the internet, any web addresses or links contained in this book may have changed since publication and may no longer be valid.

RESOURCES FOR ENTREPRENEURS

General Business

- www.freshvending.com
- www.Sba.gov
- www.Franchisedirect.com
- www.Homebasedbusiness.com
- www.Inc.com
- www.Entrepreneur.com
- www.Homepartyplannetwork.com
- www.franchisegator.com
- www.startupbusiness.com
- www.greenecoservices.com
- www.business.com

Funding

- http://www.grants.gov/
- www.funded.com/
- http://www.businessfinance.com/startup-funding

Empower Yourself through Education

www.50States.com/college/ Universities

START BY OFFERING FREELANCE SERVICES

An excellent and low-risk way to test a new business idea, especially if it's a service, is by freelancing. Not only does this give you the opportunity to test the market and do research, but you can also generate a secondary income.

As much as we might not like it, money does make the world go 'round. It expands your options and what you're able to do for your family, now and in the future. If you have a marketable talent, establishing a freelance offering is a perfect way of getting things off the ground. The advent of the World Wide Web the proliferation of mobile devices and high-speed internet, means that you can offer your services while working from home.

Benefits of home-based businesses:

- No additional facility overhead
- More flexibility in when you work

- Ability to multitask alongside home-life responsibilities
- Global audience
- Potential customers have 24/7 access to information about your services

Establishing a side business out of your home offers the least expensive method for starting up. Whether you're offering a service (freelancing) or selling products, there are solutions and platforms designed to provide you with the infrastructure needed to conduct business. More importantly, the well-established providers, bring potential customers right to you! This allows you to experiment with your offerings to prospective buyers without advertising costs. Word of caution, doing business online is as equally fabulous as it is fraught with pitfalls from being scammed. NEVER provide credit card or banking information, pay for or subscribe to a service to do business, without conducting a thorough investigation.

OPPORTUNITIES FOR FREELANCERS

While the services listed below are legitimate, credible, and have been around for years, you can find a horror story from someone about each one. Start cautiously, adhere to their guidelines, and approach all customers with a healthy skepticism.

- Fiverr - offer a variety of services online where it costs you nothing to get started. Don't be intimidated by the enforced introductory $5 price point. It's about learning to position that offering as a teaser. Fiverr takes a percentage of your revenue.

- Upwork - offer a variety of services by bidding for projects their customers have listed. Focus on verified customers and projects where the payment has also been verified to reduce the chance of not being paid. Upwork takes a percentage of your revenue.
- Freelancer - offer service packages and bid on work. Volume and popularity are not as large as Fiverr or Upwork. Many of the offerings are more like short-term contract positions than building a business or online brand.
- Uber or Lyft - categorized as freelance because you're using your own vehicle, working the hours you choose and covering the areas you want. You're essentially a freelance taxi driver.

SELLING MERCHANDISE

A whopping 79% of Americans now shop online. That's a HUGE potential market. Now consider that when you're selling online, your audience is global in most cases. There's a lot to be said for small online retailers. If this is something of interest to you, you'll have your work cut out looking for merchandise you can buy at wholesale and sell for retail. There's also the risk of purchasing merchandise and not being able to sell it at all.

For that reason, many who start this type of business, prefer to do drop shipping. Essentially, this means you don't purchase the merchandise until you have a paying customer in hand, and the merchandise goes from the procurer/shipper to the customer. You never touch the merchandise. T-Shirts, personalized clothing, and accessories, are all popular in the drop shipping market.

- Amazon is the biggest platform currently available to drop shippers, but you'll need to apply for their program. As you can imagine, there's a bit of a wait to have your account processed with tens of thousands of applicants daily. It requires a monthly fee and a percentage of your revenue.
- Establishing your own website is an alternative to Amazon but driving traffic to your site aka potential customers, will require an advertising and marketing budget. Most people will also have to pay someone to set up a professional looking website. Check website designers on Fiverr.
- Facebook Business Page is often used as the vehicle by which you sell drop-shipping merchandise. Here you can use your family and friends to help promote your business.

OTHER TYPES OF MERCHANDISE

If you're crafty or love sniffing out one of a kind bargains, Etsy and eBay might be a good fit. On the opposite spectrum from drop shipping, here the merchandise is in your hands - you have inventory of something to sell.

169

- Etsy - If you sew, paint, make jewelry or anything else handmade, Etsy has come into the big time. They've dressed up their once humble facade as "crafters only" to curating high-end unique merchandise. Like Fiverr or Amazon, they already have a huge customer base of potential customers for you, without you having to spend anything on advertising. You pay a nominal fee for listing items for sale and a percentage of the revenue.
- eBay - Not quite the kind of online bargains it was in its heyday, there are still opportunities to buy low and sell higher. However, these days, it requires a lot more research and savviness on your part to pick the right products to sell.

FIND YOUR DREAM JOB

Okay, so, we can't all have a dream job the moment we want one. However, that doesn't mean you have to stay stuck in a dead-end profession that's not at all fulfilling. We all need to be gainfully employed and you may be in an area with fewer choices. Regardless, you should always be on the lookout for more and better. It doesn't matter if it takes a long time to find it when it's that or staying put. Many jobs are filled by employee referrals or at least by getting a jump on the competition by hearing about the position before it's publicly posted. If you're looking to change jobs or have an interest in working for a specific company, be sure to let family, friends, and acquaintances know. Let your social network give you a leg up in finding that new job opportunity.

Times have changed. If you haven't looked for a job in many years, the internet has had a significant impact on job searching. Every large company has a web presence, most with a section for career opportunities. Many employers won't even take applications in person. You can only apply online. Similarly, employment agencies and related services have online application processes too. Here are a few of the more popular job search platforms:

LinkedIn.com
Careerbuilder.com
Oddskills.com
Simplyhired.com
Indeed.com
Monster.com
Snagajob.com
Craigslist.com

CHAPTER 21
GAIN CONTROL OF YOUR FINANCES

"IF YOU LIVE long enough, Life will test you. The top four reasons for financial instability are a loss of job, death, sickness and divorce. Lifestyle change can occur quickly; always be prepared for the 'what if?' There are specific things individuals and couples should have in place. My advice is: Review life and disability policies annually. Make certain you have a Living Will and a Will or Trust. In a two-income household, the goal should be to live off one income and save the other. Always keep a 'just-in-case' account."

—**Marilyn Logan, Financial Expert, "The Money Lady"**

IT HAPPENS TO THE BEST OF US

Although we'll be discussing the basics of financial management that applies to most any person or situation, you should always seek the advice of a professional before making changes to how you manage your money. The information provided is for educational purposes only. The more control you have over your finances, the more control you have over your life.

Being a slave to a paycheck, credit card, lender, etc., narrows your choices to only the options that will satisfy the above entities. Financial independence is a core component of freedom. No, that doesn't mean you must be independently wealthy. It means that, barring extraordinary circumstances, no single entity or event can destroy your financial health. When you're living paycheck to paycheck, you are essentially, at the mercy of your current employer. If your car breaking down means not paying your rent or mortgage, you're at the mercy of a vehicle. If being sick and on disability for a period, means you can't pay most of your bills, you're at the mercy of your body and better be praying you never break a leg. There's no shame in any of these scenarios. Life happens. We are not in control of many of life's events. The only shame is not laying out a plan for better.

Very few of us are financial planners. Still, you don't have to do this on your own. The first step for regaining control of any situation is having information. Followed by using that information to define changes. And lastly, by following through with the changes, monitoring progress and adjusting the plan as necessary. Know that there are easy to use applications available for minimal costs that can help you see how you spend your money, create a new plan, and monitor the results.

Here are a few:

- Quicken—has been around for many years, is easy to use and incorporates features for entrepreneurs.
- Mint – a very popular free online budgeting and

expense-tracking software.
- You Need A Budget (YNAB for short) is built on the zero-based budgeting principle that's based on allocating every dollar you earn to a specific purpose.

IT TAKES TIME

Don't be intimidated by this topic. It's an essential skill set for everyone. It is one that honestly, we should start teaching to our children when they're young. Just trying to wrap your hands and mind around everything that makes up your household financial world, can be a bit overwhelming. For this reason, seeking the help of a financial planner can be a solution to help you to get a handle on it. The one thing I recently read that has made my overall outlook on finances more exciting is that financial planning is not only about money but about finding the best way to finance what you want out of life. It doesn't matter if what you want is spending more time with your family, traveling, changing careers, paying off debt, or buying a house. Financial planning requires you to know where you are and how to get where you want to go. Now, these are concrete items I can relate to and get excited about.

I also read that it seems that the biggest problem most people face with their finances is that they talk about them all the time but they do not organize their financial data, and so they don't know where they stand at any given time.

BASIC STEPS TO REGAIN CONTROL

The first step to getting on top of your finances is to get organized. Create a system where all your financial papers and bills are together for easy reference so that you can stay on top of them. Organizing your finances includes everything from putting your bills in order and paying your bills on time to knowing where your auto and life insurance policies are. If your bills are organized so that you know what is due then there is a better chance of properly budgeting the money and paying them on time.

Next, make sure you are not spending more than you make. You can do this by tracking every penny of your spending in a notebook or a computer-based program. It sounds hard but you need to do this to get an idea of where your money is going. You will be surprised at how much of your money gets eaten up by trivial purchases. We always hear people say that they could get out of their financial hole if they just made a little more money, but the truth is that the more we make, the more we spend. We make a conscious decision to provide our kids with cell phones that have unlimited data plans and allow them to wear the $120 tennis shoes or jeans. Take a hard look at where your money goes and where you could cut back. Remember you should also put some of that paycheck into savings for emergencies and retirement.

Keep track and see that your Net Worth is growing. Take what you own (Assets,) minus, what you owe (Liabilities) to get your Net Worth. Keep track of this from year to year to see how it is growing. As you pay off loans, your liabilities will decrease while your assets increase.

Track your debt to income ratio. This shows how much of your income goes directly to paying your debt, what you owe. To get this ratio; take what you owe, your debt (car, mortgage, student loans, credit card debt. etc.) and divide it by your income. This ratio should be around 30% (.30) when you are younger and move towards zero (0) as you approach retirement. If your ratio is too high, then figure out a plan to pay off some of that debt and hold back on taking out any new debt until your ratio falls in line.

Know your savings rate. As you prepare for retirement, and it's never too early to start, you should consistently put something away into savings. A target rate to strive for is a savings rate of 15% of your income. If this is more than you can afford at this point, then shoot for 10% or even 5%. The important thing is that you consistently put something away as retirement will be here faster than you think. If your kids have moved out of the house, you should increase your savings to 20 or 25%.

Keep track of your finances and remember you are making conscious decisions on where your money goes. Cut back in some areas so that you can have money for the things that are truly important to you.

MEANING OF FINANCIAL HEALTH

Financial Health refers to the condition of a person's finances. Financial health will differ from person to person. To one person being financially healthy may mean having a $250,000 college fund for each of their kids while to someone else it may mean putting away $200 a month for retirement, saving $3,000 for a down payment on a car or staying out of bankruptcy.

Wherever you may fall here are some guidelines that can help you evaluate your financial health. This information comes from Money Magazine and CNN Money.

- Housing Cost - Your housing cost should not be more than 28% of your gross income.
- Debt- Your total debt should not exceed 36% of your gross income.
- Emergency Savings - At minimum three months' worth of living expenses should be kept in a savings account or high-yield money-market fund for emergencies. You need to increase this to six months' worth, if you rely on one income or have kids.
- Life Insurance - Your life insurance should replace at least five years of your salary. If you have children or large amounts of debt you may need as much as 10 years.
- Retirement Savings - How much you need in retirement savings depends on several factors: At what age are you planning on retiring? How long you will live. How much will your nest egg continue to grow? How much of your "pre-retirement income" will you continue to draw, through some sort of pension plan, after you stop working?
- When you work on a plan using 65 as your retirement age. Make sure you contribute the

maximum allowed to any 401K plan at work and take advantage of tax-deferred retirement accounts.

- Diversification - Stocks can provide good growth but as the market has shown lately poses plenty of risks. Bonds offer more stability. If you are saving for retirement and want a quick idea of what percentage of your portfolio should be in stocks, subtract your age from 110.
- Company Stock - Holding too much of any one stock can be risky. It is best to keep it below 10%.

BUYING SOMETHING ON YOUR OWN

Not being involved in financial matters has its downside. Often, only one person handles the financial matters. In some relationships when a car or home is purchased, only one name goes on the note. There's a single person handling the finances and keeping things in order. It seems nice because not everyone likes to deal with these things but the person who does not have a basic understanding of how things are kept running in the household, are possibly putting themselves in a difficult position. What happens if they're in a position where they can't continue that responsibility? How do the others, suddenly thrust into taking ownership, make sound decisions, not having been involved in the past?

A colleague of mine recently tried to go out on her own to purchase a vehicle. Even though she and her husband had purchased a house and several cars in the past, she had never been part of the purchasing process.

The finance officer at the dealership was impressed with her steady job and income as well as the one department store credit card that she had made timely payments on over the last year. But all this did not stop him from turning her away on the grounds of lack of credit and payment history in her name.

I always thought the less I owed others, the better. It seems that in our credit-based society this is not always the case. If you do not owe at least a handful of people something and cannot show a history of timely payments, then you are not a good credit risk. To ensure you are not left out in the cold if you ever had to take care of financial matters on your own be sure you are involved in all financial matters around your home now.

When purchasing a house or a car be sure that your name is on the contract next to your mates. Having a savings and checking account in your name may not help your credit score, but it can establish a history of a good relationship with a bank that may then be willing to cover you for a loan.

Have a credit card, small furniture loan and some of the utilities in your name. Having your name on these credit cards, loans, and utilities makes you accountable and responsible. Be sure that payments are always made on time, as bad credit may be even harder to overcome than no credit.

Take charge of getting involved in your household finances. Make it a family activity and share a basic understanding of these things with your children at a young age. This will at the same time prepare you to better handle financial matters on your own whether in a relationship or not. There is nothing worse than feeling trapped in a dead relationship because your financial existence depends solely on someone else. Maybe you have heard the expression "Be sure to stash some money away in case of a rainy day." One thing I have learned is, in life, you cannot plan all outcomes. Some things catch you by surprise. Now the difference here for the person that has this stash and one who does not is you will have options. Initially, I felt this could undermine the unity in the relationship, and this could be conveyed as you have no trust in the relationship and could make one feel they are being dishonest.

But, let's explore this. What makes it dishonest? The dishonesty would be in a secret not the fact that you have personal savings. Question, why does it have to be a secret? You are adults. Keep in mind many households today are two income households. It only makes sense for there to be a joint account to manage family affairs and individual accounts for more personal needs.

WHY MONEY MATTERS

There are many things to consider before turning in your briefcase. Money matters affect us in many ways. The following information, from an article written by Laurie PK of Quips and Tips for Money and Love, helps us understand that we need to take ownership of our finances.

Are your debts, credit cards, or student loans controlling you or are you controlling them? Are your finances a source of freedom or a cause of stress? The following signs of a financially healthy woman will help you figure out if you are in control of your money or if you need to take control of your money. "Women need to develop a healthy, honest relationship with our money," says financial guru Suze Orman. "And we have to see this relationship as a reflection of our relationship with ourselves."

In other words, our financial lives (mortgage payments, credit card debt, emergency savings fund, monthly budget, etc.) are part of who we are as women. The serious debt or extreme wealth in our finances directly affects our emotional, physical, and spiritual lives.

FIVE SIGNS OF SOUND FINANCES

1. Financially healthy people are aware of their "money personalities." Did your parents invest in real estate, a secure low-interest savings account, and mutual funds – or did they struggle with debt? Your saving and spending habits, investment style, attitude about money, and financial perspective is shaped in part by the way your parents treated money in your childhood. Your money personality directly affects your relationship with money – and the more self-aware you are, the more financial independence you'll enjoy.

2. Financially healthy people take risks. A financial risk doesn't necessarily mean investing $10,000 in a friend's new business or charging a $2,500-dollar dress to a maxed-out credit card. Taking smart financial risks includes investing in your career by going back to school full or part-time, taking a mortgage on a small piece of real estate, or exploring ways to earn money from your hobby.

A smart financial risk can even be deciding if it's a good idea to pay off your mortgage early (because sometimes it's not!).

3. Financially healthy people have their own checking, savings, or credit card accounts. So many readers make comments on my "Quips and Tips for Achieving Your Goals" blog about how they want to leave their common-law or married husbands but can't because they have no money to support themselves. Having a separate checking or savings account is the most basic sign of a financially independent woman … and yet many women don't have their own source of money.

4. Financially healthy people have both individual and couple money goals. Our goal as a married couple is to pay off the mortgage within a few months; my goal as a businesswoman is to earn $2,500 per month from my blogs. My husband has his own financial goals, mostly related to investing money in stocks and bonds. For a woman to have financial independence, she needs to have goals that are separate from her partner's. If you and your partner see money differently, you might find Dealing with Different Money Personalities as a Couple helpful!

5. Financially healthy people understand basic personal finance. This is why books about money for women are important! I can't describe retirement investing, compound and simple interest rates, living trusts, home insurance, income tax strategies, etc. here—but a basic understanding of money is crucial for everyone.

The more you know about basic personal finance, the more independent you'll be.

"Remember to stay involved with your money and to nurture a healthy relationship with it, for what happens to your money affects the quality of your life and the lives of all those you love."
—Suze Orman

The original author of this article, *Five Signs of Financial Independence,* is Laurie Pawlik-Kienlen. She is a full-time writer and blogger and created the "Quips and Tips" blog.

What the Bible says about finances:

"And my God will meet all your needs according to the riches of his glory in Christ Jesus" (Philippians 4:19 NIV).

"Whoever loves money never has enough; whoever loves wealth is never satisfied with their income. This too is meaningless" (Ecclesiastes 5:10 NIV).

CHAPTER 22
WHAT IS LOVE?

IS LOVE THE REASON we want a relationship? What are we looking to accomplish? Who does not want to feel or have LOVE?

What is Love to You?

_____

_____

What is God's Love to You?

_____

_____

Here are seven commonly considered types of love:

1. Agape—Love of the soul (God's Love)
2. Eros - Love of the body
3. Philia - Love of mind
4. Ludus - Playful love
5. Pragma - Longstanding love
6. Philautia - Love of the self
7. Storge - Love of family

CHAPTER 23

INTRODUCTION TO RELATIONSHIPS

"EMPOWERMENT COMES FROM LEARNING the truth about yourself. Now it's time to learn what makes you tick. Examine the factors in your past that shaped your frame of reference. Without that information, the past has the power to hold your future hostage. Half of the problem in getting your head on straight is having a scant knowledge of why you're the way you are. You are a complex being. Getting acquainted with yourself is a key factor in someone else getting to know you. Transparency is an attractive quality. The beauty of life is that nobody is perfect. Our flaws are like the grooves of a key. They fashion us to fit with certain people. Not everyone is going to like you. Thank God for that. That in itself gives value to the people who love and accept you for who and what you are."

—Dr. D. Ivan Young, Certified Master Coach And Relationship Expert

Yes, relationships are a part of life, but it is so important that you have a true sense of who you are to understand who you can be in a relationship. And know when you are compromising yourself past who you were created to be. At the end of the day, before approaching a relationship, you need to be happy with you in or out of a relationship.

A relationship should not define you. That is why it is so important to know who you are and what you want without compromising who you were created to be. Having a life of your own to bring to a relationship is important. If you currently do not have one. Get one! Through these exploratory exercises in this book, I hope you will begin to see how important your life truly is and begin to live your best life and really understand how valuable your life is.

Think of yourself as one of the actual talents that was talked about in the parable in Matthew 25-14-30. In my research, I found that these talents typically weighed from about 33 kg (75 pounds) varying from 20 to 40 kg. A 33 kg is worth about $1.25 million. Surely God created you with even more value, and what did you do with it? You buried it.

THE MERGER

Establishing who you are before entering into a relationship is beneficial. Many people say 50/50 makes a great relationship. That means you are only taking a half of person into it. I am sorry to report that in this case, two halves do not make a whole when it comes to relationships. Two complete people entering a relationship makes 100% because you are not going into that relationship with the expectation of that person making you complete. You should already be at 100% yourself. The other part of that is, if the relationship takes away from your 100%, it is not healthy either. A relationship should only enhance who you already are. Kind of like makeup was designed to enhance what is already there. I know you are probably thinking that is what makeup was designed to do, however, today some people are creating a whole new image with contouring and other techniques. I am not going to touch that. I hope even those people are at least satisfied with who they are on the inside. Let's look at some examples of two different relationship dynamics. One is an example of a healthy relationship, the other not so happy.

Relationship Types

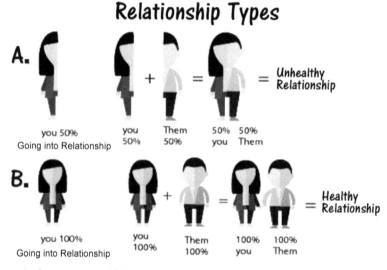

A.

you 50%
Going into Relationship

you 50% + Them 50% = 50% you 50% Them = Unhealthy Relationship

B.

you 100%
Going into Relationship

you 100% + Them 100% = 100% you 100% Them = Healthy Relationship

A. Example of a Unhealthy Relationship

You can see that in this example nothing is whole.

1. Two different people can not make a whole person.

2. It appears you are looking for someone to complete you.

3. Here you see one person could lose their identity if full assimilation happens.

4. Adding someone else's half to you will change who you were created to be.

B. Example of a Healthy Relationship

Here you can see two whole people equals a Healthy Relationship.

1. Each person here has their own existence and identity.

2. There is a better chance that this couple will enhance each other.

3. They understand the importance of not allowing anyone to subtract from their 100%.

CHAPTER 24
GO DEEPER

WHEN IT COMES TO DATING, don't stop at, "Do you want kids?" We all know the basic questions we ask when considering someone to date or marry. Here are more in-depth questions. Be sure you have your own answers to these.

1. How old are you?

   _____

   _____

2. What do you do for a living?

   _____

   _____

3. Where do you live?

   _____

   _____

4. What are your goals?

   _____

5. Where do you see yourself in five years?

6. Are you close to your family?

7. What are your religious beliefs?

8. Do you want kids and how many do you want?

Beyond the basic questions, there are others that should be given serious consideration.

1. How do you want to raise your kids?

2. What is the hierarchy (order) for a family? (God, Mate, Children)

3. How were you raised?

_____

_____

4. If you have different religious backgrounds, ask how this will affect the children.

_____

_____

5. What role do you expect to play in parenting?

_____

_____

6.
What role do you expect me to play in parenting?

_____

_____

7. Do you feel it is the woman's responsibility to take care of the kids while the man's responsibility is to bring home the bacon?

_____

_____

8. Would you expect me to work outside of the home? ... Or ... Would you expect me to give up my career to raise the kids?

_____

_____

9. Do you think it is important to continue to nurture a marriage while raising a family or will the marriage be put on hold until the kids are off on their own?

_____

10. Do you think date nights and vacations are important to a relationship?

Many times, a relationship is fine until children come along, then people suddenly realize they have two very different ideas on how they want to raise them. Real problems can arise from those differences. The main problem comes from the fact that those children are equally yours (50/50). What you now have is a power struggle over whose methods and ideas of child-rearing are best for the kids. This issue has and will cost a lot of heartache and marriages. Guess who is the biggest loser? Yes, the children. They have two parents that are on different pages when it comes to how to raise them. That means they have two parents that send different messages and struggle to get along.

Please take this advice and add a few questions to your list for the sake of your future family. Overall, you want to ensure:

- You're dealing with someone who exhibits healthy companion qualities that promote self-worth.
- You're with someone who supports your dreams and aspirations and is willing to help you cultivate your gifts and talents.
- It's someone who appreciates you for who you are, imperfections and all.

CHAPTER 25

DON'T IGNORE RED FLAGS

HERE ARE 11 RED FLAGS that should make you take a step back and analyze your relationship a little closer. Some of these Red Flags we found through research while others we encountered ourselves.

1. Does the man/woman of your dreams treat you like a king/queen but shows little respect for others in their life? If they show disrespect to their parents and friends, then you may need to consider that their level of respect for you will change the longer you are together. If part of his personality is to disrespect the people in his life, then don't expect him to treat you any differently as your relationship progresses.

2. You have been seeing this person for a while, and you enjoy going out to dinner and dancing or just hanging out at your place. Let a red flag go up if you are never invited to or end up at their place. What are they hiding? Could it be that they

have a family or another relationship? Are they a slob or do they live in their mom's basement? You may want to look closer and see why you have never been invited.

3. Where do you rank on their priority list? If you are constantly down below their work, friends, family, and dog, then you may want to consider that a red flag. If there is a family event that they must go to and therefore break a date, you might want to ask why you could not go along. If you are continually pushed to the bottom of the stack, you are either not that important to them or they may be hiding another part of their life from you. Either way, the red flag should be drawing your attention.

4. Any sign of abuse (emotional or physical) is a red flag. Do not make excuses for how you are to blame or that there are certain factors in their life right now that set them off. If there is physical or emotional abuse chances are that they will continue and even escalate. If they raise their hand at you even if it does not connect it is time to get out, no excuses.

5. Does the person you have seen for two weeks say what everyone wants to hear? Do their words seem like they're out of a movie? Let a red flag go up when the words you hear seem rehearsed because maybe they are rehearsed. Consider the fact that if they are rehearsed, this is probably not the first time they used this approach and chances are it won't be the last.

6. Does the person you are seeing seem perfect? Asks you about yourself and listens for hours.

Have they paid attention and know what you like to eat and drink? Have they memorized and know your work schedule better than you do so they surprise you by picking you up for that late lunch you were taking today. If this person seems too good to be true, they probably are so let the red flag go up. During the beginning stages of dating a person will send his proxy in place of them self. The proxy will act like the perfect person while trying to impress you with what you want to see. This proxy opens doors, pulls out chairs and remembers the name of the person you just had a conflict with at work. The proxy sticks around for 60 to 90 days. If you get through the first three months then chances are you will start to see the real person. So, take your time and let the relationship progress slowly. Don't rush into moving in together or getting engaged. Take the time to let the real person come out and then determine if they are a keeper or not.

7. History does matter. When you first get to know someone ask about their past relationships; how long they lasted and why they broke it off. Past patterns should send up red flags. Have they been in and out of relationships constantly starting a new one before they have gotten over the last one? Do they blame their exes for everything or do they take some ownership of what happened in past relationships?

8. Does your man/woman call their mother before every one of your dates to let her know what he or she is wearing and where the two of you will be? Did they cancel last Saturday's dinner

because their mom needed them to come over to keep her company? Do they still live at home? Let a red flag go up that you may have a mama's boy or daddy's girl on your hands. Yes, caring for their parents may be sweet but if they are helping them decide where to take you, then you may be in trouble. Only if they are caring for their elderly parent by letting them live in their house should they need to check up on them during the evening. Remember if they are overly attached and influenced by their parents during your dating days then don't expect that to change if you end up marrying them. It will be hard for you to compete with their parents who will surely let you know how you should be treating their child and raising their grandkids.

9. If someone moves quickly at progressing your relationship let that be a red flag. If you have had only a couple of dates and now you are flying fast, strictly on emotions, spending time with them 24/7 and not having any other outside life you might want to step back and take a minute to evaluate the situation. They may be trying to woo you and pull you into a relationship by making your head spin so that you do not have time to think or see the red flags. If you are with them at the expense of dropping all other outside life, you may want to slow everything down. If they are an understanding, wonderful person, then they will understand. If they react by trying to make you feel guilty or shame you into continuing at the current rate, then there may be a hidden agenda. Remember it takes a while to get to know

someone and to learn about their ins and outs. Don't let flattery, gifts or hot sex move you along faster than you intend to.

10. Are you enjoying going out dancing and partying with your mate? It is great to have a good time and have a drink or two when you go out but if your mate must have just one more before you go or gets angry that you are even questioning why they want another drink then you may consider that as a red flag. If you see any sign of alcohol abuse or drug use you may want to turn and run. Regularly drinking and getting drunk is not having a good time. It can be a serious problem that can even turn deadly if they end up driving after a night out.

11. What could be wrong with a mate who is willing to spend their money on new clothes for you, the mate who treats you like a queen/king by taking you shopping or buying you gifts? Let a red flag go up if you end up with a wardrobe they like more than you. Yes, they could be influencing your purchases for personal reasons. It is a subtle way of taking control over how you dress and look while looking like the hero for taking you shopping.

On the next page, list the Red Flags you have seen and heeded or some you should have noticed and not ignored.

I recognized:

1. _____
_____
2. _____
_____
3. _____
_____
4. _____
_____
5. _____
_____

I ignored:

1. _____
2. _____
3. _____
4. _____
5. _____

The ones that should have been deal breakers:

1. _____
2. _____
3. _____
4. _____
5. _____

CHAPTER 26

HOW RELATIONSHIPS AFFECT YOUR BLUEPRINT

It's important that we cultivate the right relationships in our life. To become the people God wants us to be, it's essential that we choose the right relationships. They are extremely important because, without them, we will be unable to accomplish much.

"Iron sharpens iron, so one man sharpens another" (Proverbs 27:17).

We should pursue relationships with people who:

- Build our confidence in God as well as in ourselves.
- Encourage us when we are troubled and despondent.
- Stimulate us to reach our potential.
- Energize us when we are weary.

201

- Comfort us when we are hurting.
- Defend us when we are attacked.
- Forgive us when we make mistakes.
- Love us unconditionally.
- Confront us when we go astray.
- Hold our arms up when we are overextended.

In Exodus 17:11-12 we see the battle between the Israelites and the Amalekites. As long as Moses held up his hands, the Israelites were winning, but when he lowered them, they began to lose.

During this battle when Moses' hands grew tired, Aaron and Ur saw this and took a stone and put it under him and he sat on it, then they held his hands up—one on one side, one on the other—so that his hands remained steady till sunset.

It is good to ask ourselves if we have anyone in our life who fills the needs mentioned on this list. It is also important to discover which relationships may be deflecting us from the path of godliness. When this happens, we may have to separate from certain individuals to maintain our standards. But when separation is not an option—as when the unhealthy relationship involves a family member—we can still persevere and walk with God.

Now, let's look at the same list from a different angle: Do you do those things for others? We can determine to provide those qualities to people around us. Such relationships are among life's greatest treasures.

–Clarence P. Landry Jr.

CHAPTER 27

ESTABLISH HEALTHY FAMILY RELATIONSHIPS

ESTABLISHING HEALTHY FAMILY RELATIONSHIPS means respecting the prospective roles everyone has in your household and understanding that all relationships in your family are important and need to be nurtured and cultivated individually to form strong relationship bonds in your family. Example: You have a family of four, Mother, Father and two kids. Here are the individual relationships that should exist in this family.

Key:

Mother (m)

Father (f)

Son (s)

Daughter (d)

Here are the examples of the individual relationships that should exist in this family.

Mother (m)

m + f, m + s, m + d = Individual relationships

Father (f)

f + m, f + s, f + d = Individual relationships

Son (s)

s + f, s + m, s + d = Individual relationships

Daughter (d)

d + f, d + m, d + s = Individual relationships

Then you have the combined unit which forms the family.

= The Family Relationship

DANGERS OF A SINGLE KEY PERSON

There's a hidden danger in aligning your family so that a single key person exists. In all individual relationships, each person must take an active role to build, grow and nurture them. It is not the role of one Key person in the family to simulate a link between relationships other than their own. If this happens, this gives a false sense that these other family relationships even exist.

Why pass a message through a family member in your household, and miss the opportunity to connect directly with that individual and have dialogue and a direct response? (Cut out the middleman whenever possible)

WHY IT'S A BAD IDEA

Awkwardness could occur when the family is going to do something, and that key person is not involved. As this pertains to parenting, a lot of times, it will appear that the Key person knows more about what is going on with everyone and this could cause one parent to feel left out. But, the Key person only knows more because they are engaged and connected with each person. (There is not a conspiracy going on).

It's important to spend quality time in all of the relationships. Many couples take vacations together as a couple but once they have children, some couples decide to put their relationship on hold while they raise their children. They plan to pick it back up once the kids graduate from high school. Is this a good or bad thing? You might commend them and say wow that is quite a sacrifice. And you would be right. But, why would you want to sacrifice the very relationship that produced these kids out of love and togetherness in the first place?

For many couples, this happens, and it is not intentional at all. Sometimes the demands of childrearing, work and life have the couple acting like two ships passing in the night. Then the day comes when the children leave home for college or to pursue their own lives. Now you have two strangers left at home. You may be thinking doesn't absence make the heart fonder? Well statistics say the absence of the relationship make the heart forget. Some couples look at this shift as an opportunity to now focus on the only life they have known other than their children's, their own, instead of seeing this as a time to rebirth their relationship and chart a new course together.

THERE ARE NO GUARANTEES

In life, there are not many guarantees. But maybe a chance to decrease the odds would be worth the effort. First, we need to understand the healthy order of the family should be the mate and then the children for this reason. Here are a few items to consider for an Empty Nest Survival Plan.

- Keep God in the center.
- Honor this relationship.
- Respect each other.
- Do not take each other for granted.
- Plan date nights.
- Vacation without the children.
- Continue to make plans for your future together.
- Remember what attracted you to your mate in the first place. After all, they were your choice, and nobody is perfect.
- Work as a team in everything (raising your family and managing your household).
- Treat each other as best friends protect each other and hold their trust as an extension of your own.

CHAPTER 28
FORGIVENESS IS FOR YOU

HAVE YOU EVER NOTICED that when you carry a grudge or feel the way about something or toward someone, it stays at the top of your mind for you and it takes up a lot of your time and energy and emotions?

This is a form of stress. Well, the irony is more times than not the other person doesn't even know how you feel or they have forgotten about it and moved past it. So how does the way you feel hurt or affect them or make them suffer? It doesn't. By forgiving them, it will help you move on and not continue to live with the stress of un-forgiveness.

UNEXPLAINED LAPSES IN RELATIONSHIPS

Let's look at forgiveness and transitioning through unexplained lapses in a relationship.

- **Definition of Irreconcilable Differences**
  Substantial incompatibility between marriage

partners that is a broad ground for no-fault divorce.

- **Definition of Irretrievable Breakdown of the Marriage**
  A broad ground for divorce that is predicated on the development of incompatibility between marriage partners that is used in many states as the sole ground of no-fault divorce–called also an irremediable breakdown of the marriage or irretrievable breakdown.

Many of us have heard of expressions like growing apart and empty nest syndrome. When some people hear of irreconcilable differences, many people say to themselves *who does that?* What a cop out and lastly does that really happen? In 1997, 80% of divorces were categorized as due to irreconcilable differences.

Based on these statistics, we can see it really does happen, and this 80% shows us it happens a lot. I am sure all situations are different. But, I believe if neither person disrespects their marriage or each other, it is a greater possibility that they can make a smooth transition. For many making this decision, the factor is "You only get one life, and life is too short to be unhappy."

By no means am I soliciting divorce. I believe the more vital issue is quality of life. There are physical and mental factors that drive this outcome. By taking these things into consideration, the quality of one's health and emotional stability sometimes warrants this solution. These reasons do not lessen the blow, hurt and anger and disappointment are still the same.

But, by choosing forgiveness over the disappointment and hurt it could lend to a better possibility of gaining a new level of respect for one another. For many couples, once a mutual understanding of the relationship is reached, strangely enough, they tend to notice how they are more able to enjoy the simple mutual things such as conversations and common courtesy. This maturity in a couple's transition can create grounds for neutral exchange without any toxicity. That would only hinder the transition process and breed negativity blame and resentment and put their life on hold.

If at the beginning of this relationship there was a friendship that the foundation was built on, they will notice that with all that they have been through, the ups/downs, struggle and hurt the foundation still exists. I am convinced that spending time complaining about an ex is not time spent well. It is simply time spent spinning. You cannot move into your new chapter because you have not ended or come to terms with the other. This is a choice. It is not easy, but it is productive and healthy.

Always remember, that at one time, this person was your choice, good, bad, or indifferent. Remembering what you loved about them i is especially important if you have children. Bashing anyone is not healthy for anyone. Many times, we spend time and energy reflecting and harboring anger against someone, hoping they feel the hurt and pain we feel. Unfortunately, most of the time that is not the case. The person has moved on with their life and probably have not gave another thought to that situation. What a waste of your time, effort, and energy.

Many people were in a committed relationship for years and now must learn to find comfort and peace in their singleness. It's kind of like turning on the TV for noise. Imagine never having experienced silence for many years and always having someone around then all of the sudden that's gone. You can't turn on the TV for noise in this case. You must learn to appreciate the benefits of this silence and think and plan again solely for yourself. This silence also gives you clarity and opportunity to hear from God and allows you to tap into the whole new level of awareness and faith.

It is also important that you forgive yourself if you are carrying around personal disappointment, blame, or hurt. Forgive yourself for allowing yourself to be positioned in a place where you disappeared from and move on.

What can opening a new chapter look like? It can look bright and be filled with self-love, self-expression and fulfillment. It feels both warm and familiar but new all at the same time. When I speak of familiar, I mean remnants of untainted visions without someone else's input or direction.

If God is the Potter and we are the clay, we must remember we are already loaded into something beautifully and wonderfully made, His creation. This is proof that we should not let anyone else mold us. Even as parents our job is only to train, instill, protect, provide, and\ guide ... not to mold.

HOW WILL YOU KNOW WHEN YOU ARRIVE?

How will you know you have arrived if you do not know who you are or where you are going or why? Once you experience The Awakening, and desire to be who you were created and purposed to be, you can no longer return to being that passive person you were before. The previous position or classification you held, won't work. If you are in a relationship, this is a time where you will need to renegotiate the relationship and find common ground. First and foremost the love for one another will be even better if you both share the love for God. Reestablish this relationship and chart the path for a healthy, supportive, loving, and growing relationship. The old passive you is gone and is not coming back.

As a young woman I look back and I understand where my initial example of being a woman, a mom, and a wife was formed. I was what I saw in my household and as a young woman I had nothing to gauge to determine if this was normal or healthy. Some say there are generational curses for behavior such as having children out of wedlock and grown people still living with their parents. I believe there is also a generational curse for not knowing you can be who you were created to be in spite of the roles people expect of you. I think this starts with self-esteem and knowing your self-worth early as a child. You should know you have a purpose in this life even if at times you do not know what that may entail. We need to understand the many roles and responsibilities life has for us.

Number one, we have a responsibility to God. Secondly, we have a responsibility to ourselves to live our best life. Our third responsibility is to our mates and our children. Fourthly, it is to our extended family and fifthly it is to our community. We must find a way to satisfy these areas without losing our self in the process. Some people say most life goals are to go one step better than our parents. That's the first problem; we are not our parents so why do we think one step better will complete us when their steps had nothing to do with us, our personalities, likes or dislikes.

If you have never seen an example of a healthy relationship, you will not know what is healthy and what is not healthy. Our exposure to the relationships around us come into play in our ideas of a healthy relationship. But always remember you are complete with or without a relationship. You can be accomplished in a career and have many degrees and still die with your purpose unfulfilled. Let's fight this epidemic of passive assimilation with fulfilled dreams and purpose and pay forward this understanding so we can be those healthy examples in someone's life.

Years ago, during this journey, the Lord gave me this pledge, and I have had the pleasure of sharing it with many people. Please recite it for yourself and share it with others.

The ME Pledge

I can serve God and my family while making a contribution to the world.
I can do this without losing myself, my dreams, my passions, my visions and my purpose.
I can do this because these things are important to me.
I will do this because, these are the things that make me, ME.
I have no need to assimilate into anyone else's life or dreams.
For this is my life, and I was created with my own purpose, and that is enough for ME.

—**Sonyia Graham**

CHAPTER 29

DON'T NORMALIZE DYSFUNCTION

IT IS ESSENTIAL TO expose and address any dysfunction in your relationship and household. Your children see it, hear it, and in many cases are affected by it. You owe them the opportunity to communicate it and process it correctly. Doing so will teach them healthy communication skills and give them a chance to express how it affected them. It could even aid in their healing and give them a better chance of not repeating this dysfunction or carrying this into their adulthood.

If you do not address dysfunction, the children will be at greater risk of repeating this as the norm. This is your chance to discuss it with them and give insight on what you could have done differently considering what you now know. It shows you are not perfect therefore they will understand they do not need to aim for that standard, which could lead to them feeling like a failure in their imperfectness.

"Start children off on the way they should go, and
even when they are old they will not turn from it"
(Proverbs 22:6 NIV).

CHAPTER 30
SECRETS TO A STRONG MARRIAGE

THERE IS A LOT OF INFORMATION concerning Secrets to a Strong Marriage that is geared to what women should do for their husbands. Some things that are recommended include: Keeping him happy in the bedroom, letting go of issues when he upsets you, giving him a long passionate kiss when he leaves for work so you will be on his mind all day, putting love notes in his briefcase, and entertaining all of his conversations and being attentive to them even if you are not really interested in what he is saying. (Overview: put the needs of your husband first.) They even go as far as to say that men may not respond to this immediately but when they do ... are they saying women should not have any expectations?

The good news is that after a lot of searching, I found some secrets to a strong marriage that were targeted to both women and men. I was happy to find this because the truth is, it does take two. No matter how hard one works in a marriage, if the other is not working at it at all, it will not become a strong marriage. It will become

215

a lot of work for one and eventually it will cause a lot of resentment.

REMEMBER UNCONDITIONAL LOVE

We have been told for years that a relationship is a 50/50 give and take. Where did that come from? A relationship is supposed to be based on unconditional love, not give to get. It seems to me if both work at giving 100%, that even when one falls short, there will be an overlap. That is what give and take really means to me. When one falls short, the other fills in and we complete each other. I believe that in successful relationships both partners will give at least 60% or 70% to allow for that overlap. After all, we are human beings, not robots. Overlap is better than a gap or void.

A few tips:

- Always nurture the foundation which should be a friendship.
- Affirm that bond with trust and respect.
- Do not put the relationship on hold while you raise the children.
- For a relationship to flourish, it must continue to be nurtured like a plant. Your marriage must receive enough water and light, otherwise, it will die.

OPEN COMMUNICATION

It's important to always keep the lines of communication open and be a listening ear. That means not only wanting to be heard but to be open to the other partner and listen when they are speaking.

PATIENCE

We could all practice being more patient. It takes an active willingness to curtail knee-jerk reactions and jumping to conclusions. Stop. Listen. Consider. Respond.

- Remember what attracted you to your mate in the first place.
- Recall how that attraction made you feel.
- Continue making plans for the future.

Whether it's a short-term plan for a vacation or long-term goals towards starting a family or retirement, talk about those plans a lot; make sure you're on the same page.

PERSONAL TIME

Going back to ME Time, it's important that you each continue to maintain and nurture your individuality and core. Continue to spend time apart. Hang out with your own friends; take a weekend solo trip to visit an old friend or explore a hobby on your own. These activities not only enrich your life and give you something to bring to the marriage/relationship, they also let your heart grow a little fonder during the absence and remind you not to take for granted the time you do spend with your mate.

ROMANCE

Romance, romance, romance - never let the flame die. It won't take care of itself. We're talking about romance, not sex. That could be holding hands, cuddling, and touches throughout the day to name a few. Even if you must initiate it, show them what you want and what you like. Or just stay miserable waiting for them to figure it out!

- Do not take them for granted.
- Show them you appreciate everything they do for you and your family.
- Share the load.

If you both work outside the home, share in the house and family responsibilities and chores.

"Love is patient, love is kind. It does not envy, it does not boast, it is not proud. It does not dishonor others, it is not self-seeking, it is not easily angered, it keeps no record of wrongs"
(1 Corinthians 13:4-5 NIV).

CHAPTER 31
MARRIAGE REHABILITATION

MARRIAGE REHABILITATION IS ABOUT reconnecting with your mate. There are many negative transitive verbs to describe the dysfunction occurring—breakup, decouple, disassociate, separate, disjoin, dissever, disunite, divide, divorce, part, sever, split, uncouple, unlink, unyoke, etc. None of these describe a situation that is joyful and you should actively avoid them in your marriage.

"Love does not delight in evil but rejoices with the truth. It always protects, always trust, always hopes, always perseveres. Love never fails... ."
(1 Corinthians 13: 6-8 NIV).

"And now three remain: faith, hope and love.
But the greatest
of these is love"
(1 Corinthians 13:13).

AVOID BECOMING DISCONNECTED

Here are some ideas you can use to stay connected with your partner and strengthen your marriage.

- Make your marriage a top priority.
- Don't find time but make time to spend with one another.
- When there is conflict, deal with it by talking openly and in a caring way so conflict can be discussed and resolved.
- Don't allow resentments to build, talk to each other and stay in tune with each other's feelings. Work together and keep communication open when you are met with life's challenges, like a birth, death, or other situations. Continue to make the relationship a priority and balance it with life's other demands.

DATE NIGHT

Take a moment to give date night opportunities some thought. It's important that the needs and likes of the both of you are served by this activity. When considering options, rotate between what each partner enjoys doing. If you don't know, ask!

List the things you like to do:

_____

_____

_____

_____

_____

List the things they like to do:

_____

_____

_____

_____

CHAPTER 32

TESTIMONY OF A DEAR FRIEND

WE MUST LEARN TO empower one another and support each other. Most importantly we must learn to be proper role models for our children and young people looking to us as examples. It is not what you go through that defines you, it is how you deal with it and how you finish. Your children will remember this part the most. Live a legacy of strength and empowerment, not shame and defeat.

A dear friend inspired me and, shared this testimony with me several years ago. She is now an empty nester and has since gone on to write more books such as *Faithful Deceptions* by Melissa Ohnoutka.

By Melissa Ohnoutka

I've always loved to make up stories. As a kid, I had the usual imaginary friends and lived to be adventurous much to the despair of my poor mother I'm sure. The first time I can remember writing something of any real length was in the 7th grade. That was a way for me to escape and create new worlds where I was in control. If a book or movie didn't end like I wanted or thought it should, no problem, I rewrote it. This made for some interesting conversations with teachers when trying to do those dreaded book reports.

Fast forward a few years, okay a lot of years. We moved from my small hometown where my family lived in a small suburb outside of Houston. I knew no one. My husband's family lived an hour away on the other side of town. Throw in the surprise of finding out I was pregnant again when my first child was only ten months old, and it was almost more than I could take. I picked up a pencil and a plain spiral notebook and started my first book. Looking back now, I realize this was a way for me to relieve the stress and anxiety of worrying how on earth I was going to handle two little ones so close in age. I wrote for fun, stress relief, and the pure thrill of a watching my words turn into a story.

A little over five years and one more baby later, we'd moved again. Two girls and one active little boy now took up most of my time, and this is where it all got tricky. I knew the writing was good for me. It helped me deal with life's little speed bumps, helped me stretch my individuality and it made me feel worthy. Yes, I am a mother and a wife. And I love every precious minute. I'm so thankful for all the blessings God has given me.

I realize now, after years of struggling with guilt over wanting time to myself, that giving me hopes and dreams of my own is also one of His blessings. I have a purpose bigger than being part of a family group. I believe this is true of every member of a family. It's what makes us grow, helps us branch out and find the path that God has laid out for us.

Now that my two daughters are in high school and my son is in middle school, the choice to follow my dream is even more critical. When they are off enjoying their own lives and raising families of their own, I'll have my writing to keep me sane. Without it, I know I'd be lost. After many years of caring for them, tending to their every need and then wham! Mommy's not needed much anymore. Who made these rules anyway? The idea of them growing up still makes me cringe and tear up, but I know this is all part of life. I also understand why it's important to have something that takes me away from the chaos, even if it's only for a little while. Writing is part of who I am, and it makes me feel secure in knowing that something I love and the great friends I've made along the way will be here to encourage and support me through these ever-changing cycles. I don't feel guilty about taking time for myself anymore. It's all about finding a balance that works for everyone.

I'll admit taking that next step in my writing career has been one scary journey. The risk of putting myself out there with the fear of failure looming all around me was enough to send me screaming and running in the opposite direction. But the "what if's" were too haunting to live with. There is a quote I came across that says it all. "There is no success without failure." Don't be afraid to branch out and build a life outside your family with friends who enjoy the same things you do. The result is a happier you. And no one benefits more than your precious family. It's a plus for everyone. Hopes and dreams are gifts. Take those chances and never be afraid to dream. I'm thrilled to be selling copies every day, which I never in a million years thought possible.

Melissa published her first book, *Faithful Deceptions*, in February 2011 and has published *Shattered Souls of Innocence, Target of Betrayal, The Wicked Secrets Beneath,* and *Betrayal of the Heart*.

CHAPTER 33
IN THE TRUNK KIND OF FAITH

FOR ME, FOR THE rest of my life, I am focused on being the best me God created. I'm making a difference and positioning myself to be used by God, and I'm not doing it alone. Our Lord and Savior is with me every step of the way. God is the author and finisher. I am riding in a trunk these days while He's driving. Let me explain.

As a passenger in a car, I can see the road and may find myself giving input to the driver concerning what to watch out for and a better way to go. This navigational interference often turns into "intense fellowship" as my god-sister would say. I have learned to face my weakness straight on and admit I had not been a model passenger when God was driving.

He has had the right to say, "If you know as much as you think you know, I'm going to pull over, let you out, and let you make your own way." When that has happened, it usually has not turned out well for me and I put those experiences in my bag of lessons. But, the amazing thing about God and His love, grace and mercy is He will pull over and pick you up again and again.

At this stage in my life, I choose to ride in the trunk when He is driving so I am not tempted to help God drive. No matter how many bumps I feel in that trunk while He's driving, when He stops and opens the trunk I'm going to jump out and trust Him. No matter what I see or how difficult it may appear, or where the location is, I will jump out with confidence that is already worked out for my good. I'm going to have a confidence to do whatever it is no matter how unusual or how uncomfortable it may seem. God has always been the driver. The question is will you let Him? Maybe you thought you were behind the wheel all these years when the truth of the matter is, He loved you so much He allowed you to drive to the destination of your choices even if He did not approve.

CHAPTER 34
PUTTING IT ALL TOGETHER

WE'VE COVERED A LOT of ground. Which is a good thing on the way to discovering your Original Blueprint. Now it's time to peel away the apathy of being who others believe you are or want you to be for their sake. Even as you serve God and your community, you're meant to be who the Lord designed, sharing the talents and gifts He provided.

And yet, it's not all about you. We each bear the burden of the impact we have on the world around us. Our relationships, marriage, role as a parent or caregiver, employee or employer, community member, etc., have a lasting footprint in the lives of others.

Being the best you, also means living a life with intention that is well-managed. You are leading your life. Your life is not leading you. How you choose the people in your life, select a partner, treat your relationship, manage finances, ensure that you're mentally, physically and spiritually fit, all play significant roles in the outcome—for better or worse. A broken record will only play a broken tune, no matter how lovely the song. We all stumble and fall. The only shame in that is staying down on the ground. In addition to finding and nurturing a better you, we've discussed methods for overcoming setbacks and how important it is for future generations that we break the cycle of apathy and dysfunction that has enveloped many of us.

How do you want to be remembered by family and friends? It's time to live as a testimony of the gifts and talents God gave you. Improve where you're weak, shine where you're strong. Live and serve. Serve and live. But at the core of discovering all that is possible, you must discover your true self – and stay true to your original blueprint.

OUR SUBJECT EXPERT BIOS

Nia Abdallah

2004 Olympic silver medalist and the first U.S. woman to officially medal in Taekwondo the Olympics. In 2007 Nia received the highest honor in the martial art/Olympic sport of Taekwondo by being inducted into the Official Taekwondo Hall of Fame. She was the first martial arts athlete endorsed by NIKE. The months following her retirement, Nia became the Texas State women's head coach and started a competition team named "Team Bacho" in her hometown of Houston Texas. Her goal is to become the United States first female Taekwondo Head Olympic Coach. Nia also travels around the country teaching seminars. Nia is now sharing her message of "Living like a Champion thru BACHO." She is currently speaking to many schools, businesses, churches, and organizations on how they can be better by using the same steps it takes to become a great athlete.

Marilyn Logan

Armed with years of experience as a successful investment broker for major corporations and individuals, "The Money Lady" has an in-your-face, pull-no-punches style that sets her apart from the everyday "stuffed shirt" financial expert. Marilyn has a rare ability to tackle serious financial matters with directness and humor. And, if you take her advice seriously, you will be laughing, instead of crying, all the way to the bank! She has appeared as a financial expert on the Dr. Phil Show, The Steve Harvey Morning Radio Show, Les Brown's Chicago Speaks and the Yolanda Adams Morning Gospel Hour. Marilyn is also a staple on the popular show Great Day Houston – the city where she currently resides. She has penned numerous articles and is often quoted in money articles for local and national publications – Black Enterprise and Uzuri Magazine, to name a few. Marilyn Logan is the author of the book, *I Can't Afford to Marry You! A Guide to Understanding the True Cost of Love*. It is a financial love story based on her life with her soul-mate and financial teacher, John. Marilyn shares her experiences with television, radio, and seminar audiences across the country and lives by the simple mantra that "...less really, really, really, is more!"

Dr. D. Ivan Young, CMC

D. Ivan Young is a TEDx Speaker and Master Credentialed Expert on personality types. As one of the most notable Life Coaches in the United States, his provocative teaching style on complex relationship subjects has been hailed as remarkable by millions of fans across the country. He is a highly sought-after motivational and keynote speaker. His many accolades include being selected from over 12,500 such professionals, by D- Mars.com Business Journal in May 2016 as one of the Top 50 African American Health, Wellness and Mental Health Professionals in Metropolitan Houston. He has been featured in/on Ted X, The Huffington Post, Yahoo News Groups, Black Enterprise, Your Tango.com, Essence Magazine.Com, TV

One's Hit Program "Fatal Attraction" & Justice by Any Means," The Oxygen Networks hit program "Snapped" – Killer Couples, MSNCB, CNN, ABC, to name a few. He is the author of *Another Chance…Where Would You Be Without One?* He became an Amazon Bestseller in 2015 for his previous work *Break Up, Don't Break Down* which was termed "The Relationship Manual" by the Associated Press.

Kittie Weston-Knauer

Owner and President of KWK Enterprise, Inc., an educational consulting firm specializing in the development and implementation of charter schools. Des Moines, IA., has been racing BMX for more than 30 years and is nowhere near ready to retire. She loves racing BMX bikes. At the age of 70, she is the oldest female in the nation to race bicycle motocross. She got into the sport of BMX racing at the age of 40 in 1988, because she was so tired of seeing her oldest son, and husband, having so much fun while she stood on the sidelines cheering for them in competitions! Kittie Weston-Knauer has the best retirement strategy ever: crushing the national BMX circuit. After 33 years as a high school principal in Des Moines, Iowa, the 70-year-old BMX champion now travels all over the US to compete in bike races. "I'm just enjoying life," she says. "I worked hard so that I could retire and play. And that's what I'm doing; I'm playing." She has received accolades on and off the bike on local, state, national and international levels and been featured on The Steve Harvey Show, nytimes.com, bicycling.com, cnn.com, usabmx.com, and parade.com to name a few. She feels the greatest honor has been her continued mentoring in

Des Moines via cycling programs and activities which empowers youth with the unique opportunities to build relationships, achieve personal growth, and learn life-skills.

ABOUT THE AUTHOR

SONYIA GRAHAM WAS BORN and raised in Des Moines, Iowa. She relocated to Houston in 1987. She is the proud mother of Andrew and Victoria Graham, who represent and are her best work. She's an author and owner of Colored Mirrors Publishing, LLC, whose motto is "Written words are colored mirrors to one's soul." Sonyia believes everyone has a story and while Sonyia is excited to share the Original Blueprint Series around the world, she is equally excited about the opportunity to help others birth their stories.

In her sports management career, she had the pleasure of managing Silver Medalist Olympian Nia

Abdallah, for whom she successfully secured the first NIKE Martial Arts endorsement in 2004. As an entrepreneur, one of her companies, Mirror Perfect Marketing, Inc., was Compaq Computer Corporation's first online promotional products provider nationwide.

Sonyia is the founder of Me Time 4 Real, a Facebook woman's social organization. She loves serving and has served as a Teen Ministry Support for 10 years as well as other ministries. Sonyia also served as president of Enrichment & Brotherhood of Northwest Youth (also known as) E.B.O.N.Y. for two consecutive years. She served in service unit and troop leadership roles for Girl Scouts of San Jacinto for nine years. Her life's passion and work are to empower others worldwide to enjoy life and live their Original Blueprint on purpose. She feels her real gift is her love for people.

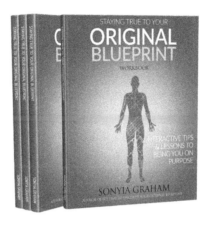

Did you know that you are a unique Original Blueprint that is wonderfully made? The amazing thing is you came into this world with your own personality, gifts, talents, and purpose. Maybe you knew that. But many do not know. Are you remaining true to yourself in everything you do? You may be that person who has all of this in perspective, if so, congratulations! To assist you in continuing on this path, I have created the workbook, *Staying True to Your Original Blueprint.*

Guess what? Believe it or not, uncovering your Original Blueprint is not the hardest part. The hardest part is staying true to your original blueprint in the first place. Life will throw many things at you. And for one reason or another, that path starts looking less clear. Now you have friendships, other relationships, family, work, school and just plain life to consider.

It is important that you keep defining and carving out your own identity in all of these areas, and remain 100% you, otherwise the epidemic of passive assimilation can overtake your true self, even in relationships, and then you may be at risk of disappearing.

Staying True to Your Original Blueprint is imperative for fulfilling God's purpose for your life. The *Staying True to Your Original Blueprint* workbook offers interactive tips and lessons to help you see your life and live your best life on purpose.

This workbook is a must have, especially for young people. The earlier they understand this the better their odds will be to beat or never have to experience passive assimilation in their lifetime. Get it for your loved ones and friends.

Other upcoming titles are *Journaling Through Your Original Blueprint* and *Let's Re-negotiate.*

—Sonyia Graham, *Author*

CPSIA information can be obtained
at www.ICGtesting.com
Printed in the USA
LVHW02s1216190718
584244LV00014B/31/P

9 781732 107816